# BY STANLEY YOUNG

A COMEDY FREELY DRAWN FROM
CHARLES DICKENS' *THE PICKWICK PAPERS*

RANDOM HOUSE • NEW YORK

FIRST PRINTING


PUBLISHED IN NEW YORK BY RANDOM HOUSE, INC., AND SIMULTANEOUSLY IN TORONTO, CANADA, BY RANDOM HOUSE OF CANADA, LIMITED

LIBRARY OF CONGRESS CATALOG CARD NUMBER: 52-13255

DESIGN: MERLE ARMITAGE



MANUFACTURED IN THE UNITED STATES OF AMERICA

FOR NANCY WILSON ROSS

MR. PICKWICK was first presented in London at the Westminster Theatre by Thane Parker, Limited, on May 15, 1952, and was produced by The Playwrights Company in New York at the Plymouth Theatre on September 17, 1952, with the following cast:

*(In order of appearance)*

| | |
|---|---|
| MR. PICKWICK | GEORGE HOWE |
| MR. TUPMAN | EARL MONTGOMERY |
| MR. SNODGRASS | ANTHONY KEMBLE COOPER |
| MR. WINKLE | DEREK TANSLEY |
| MRS. BARDELL | NORAH HOWARD |
| MRS. CLUPPINS | LUCIE LANCASTER |
| SAM WELLER | CLIVE REVILL |
| TOMMY | RICHARD CASE |
| MR. BUZFUZ | JACQUES AUBUCHON |
| MRS. WELLER | PHILIPPA BEVANS |
| MR. WELLER | LOUIS HECTOR |
| MR. STIGGINS | BASIL HOWES |
| MR. JINGLE | NIGEL GREEN |
| MARY | SARAH MARSHALL |
| MRS. LEO HUNTER | ESTELLE WINWOOD |
| JOE | C. K. ALEXANDER |
| MR. WARDLE | NEIL FITZGERALD |
| MISS EMILY WARDLE | JEAN COOKE |
| MISS ISABELLA WARDLE | DOLORES PIGOTT |
| MISS RACHEL WARDLE | NYDIA WESTMAN |
| MR. PERKER | KURT RICHARDS |
| WILBERFORCE | WALLACE ACTON |
| BAILIFF | WALLACE ACTON |
| JUSTICE | WILLIAM PODMORE |
| TURNKEY | C. K. ALEXANDER |

*Directed by* JOHN BURRELL

*Production Designed by* KATHLEEN ANKERS

# SCENES

ACT 1

SCENE I: Mr. Pickwick's Lodgings in Mrs. Bardell's House.

SCENE II: The Inn at Chatham.

SCENE III: The Garden Party at Mrs. Leo Hunter's.

ACT 2

SCENE I: The Inn at Chatham.

SCENE II: A Courtroom in London.

SCENE III: Mr. Pickwick's Quarters in Fleet Prison.

# ACT 1

# ACT 1

## SCENE I

*TIME: May, 1827.*

*SCENE: The sitting-room of* MR. SAMUEL PICKWICK'S *lodgings in Goswell Street, London. Here the Pickwick Club is assembled around a table well supplied with wine bottles and glasses. Some very gay hunting prints are on the walls. Piles of luggage stand by the door.*

*The Pickwickians appear to be as gravely concerned as clubmen usually are at important meetings. Most prominent of the group is the immortal* PICKWICK *himself, a precise and lovable little man, whose vigor seems to put a constant strain upon his tights and gaiters. On his right sits* MR. TUPMAN. *Time and feeding have ruined* TUPMAN'S *romantic figure; inch by inch his gold watch chain has disappeared in the folds of his black waistcoat, but the soul of* TUPMAN *has known no change. On the left sits* MR. SNODGRASS, *the poet, enveloped in a mysterious blue coat with a canine-skin collar, most poetic-looking. Near him lolls the sporting* MR. WINKLE *in a new green shooting coat, plaid neckerchief and closely fitting drabs. All four of the Pickwickians are dressed for travel.*

*AT THE CURTAIN:* MR. PICKWICK, *one hand gracefully concealed behind his coattails, is standing on a chair and addressing his fellow members with a glowing declamation that has engaged their full attention.* PICKWICK'S *bald head is gleaming, and his circular spectacles bob on his nose.*

PICKWICK

(*With a flourish*)

Gentlemen, I have observed that fame is dear to the heart of every man . . .

CLUB

(*Restrained cheers*)

Bravo! Bravo!

TUPMAN

What a penetrating observation!

PICKWICK

Poetic fame is dear to the heart of my friend Snodgrass . . .

(SNODGRASS *rises and bows gravely.*)

SNODGRASS

I *have* a poem here. . . .

PICKWICK

(*Interrupting*)

The fame of romantic conquest is equally dear to my friend Tupman . . .

(TUPMAN, *with difficulty, rises and bows.*)

TUPMAN

I am not a *great* lover, but . . .

PICKWICK

And the desire of earning renown in the sports of the field, the air and the water, has long been uppermost in the breast of my friend Winkle. (WINKLE *rises with a fieldpiece carelessly tucked under his arm, a fact that plainly introduces some apprehension among the others, for they applaud quickly and seat him forcibly*) As for myself, I will not deny that I, too, have been influenced by human passions . . .

TUPMAN

How revealing!

WINKLE

How honest!

PICKWICK

Possibly by human weaknesses . . .

SNODGRASS
WINKLE

No! No!

TUPMAN

Never! Never!

PICKWICK

But let me say, fellow Pickwickians, if ever the fire of self-importance broke out in my bosom, my desire to benefit the human race effectually quenched it!

(*More cheers.*)

TUPMAN

Long live Pickwick!

PICKWICK

Yet—I have enemies . . . (*Cries of "No! No!"*) Oh, yes. My scientific speculations on the "Source of the Hampstead Ponds, with Some Observations on the Theory of Tittlebats" naturally has called forth opponents. (*Cries of "Naturally" and "Down with 'em"*) But, if the fame of that treatise extends to the farthest confines of the known world, the pride with which I reflect on its authorship is as nothing compared with this—the proudest moment of my existence!

(PICKWICK *climbs down from his chair and sits. Applause. The Chairman,* MR. TUPMAN, *rises and raps his gavel for order.*)

TUPMAN

Gentlemen! Gentlemen! (*The members become quiet*) On behalf of the Pickwick Club, I extend our congratulations to our president, Mr. Samuel Pickwick, for his farewell message. It has been—most stimulating.

(*He sits. Cries of "Hear, hear!"*)

SNODGRASS

It is Mr. Pickwick who organized our club! It is Mr. Pickwick who has made the first scientific observation on Tittlebats! It is Mr. Pickwick who has given us our mottoes!

(*He sits. "Hear, hear!"*)

WINKLE

I think it fitting, on this historic occasion, that we repeat in unison the immortal quotations elected by our eminent President to guide us.

(*They hold up their mottoes and read.*)

CLUB

(*Together*)

Justice triumphs! . . . Look before you leap! . . . Consider passion!

(*They all sit gravely. A knock at the door.*)

MRS. BARDELL

(*Putting her head in*)

Beggin' your pardon, sir—there's a young man by the name of Samuel Weller askin' to see you.

PICKWICK

Ah, good. Kindly ask him to wait.

MRS. BARDELL

(*Coy*)

Is there anythin' I can do for you, sir? Some tea? Somethin' to perk you up a bit durin' your meetin'?

PICKWICK

No, thank you. We are most pleasantly—fortified, Mrs. Bardell.

(*He holds up a bottle.* MRS. BARDELL *retires, disappointed.*)

TUPMAN

Your landlady—very attractive, Pickwick.

PICKWICK

Is she? I hadn't noticed. Shall we get on with the meeting?

TUPMAN

The Chair respectfully calls for new business. (WINKLE *rises, with dignity*) The Chair recognizes the Secretary.

WINKLE

I shall read an order from the central society of the Club.

(*A pause.*)

TUPMAN

Proceed.

WINKLE

(*Acidly*)

I *am* proceeding.

TUPMAN

Continue to proceed.

WINKLE

"It is hereby sanctioned and approved by the Pickwick Club that four of our number be nominated members of a traveling society . . ." The purpose of said traveling society: To observe life!

TUPMAN

To observe life. Kindly read the conditions appertaining thereto.

(WINKLE *exchanges a worried whisper with* TUPMAN.)

WINKLE

Gentlemen, permit me to announce that this Association *cordially* recognizes the principle of every member defraying *his own traveling expenses.*

(*A pause.*)

TUPMAN

Are there any questions or remarks?

SNODGRASS

(*Rising*)

As a poet . . . (*Gentle applause*) As a writer of some volume, I am wondering who will pay the *postage* of our letters back to the society in London.

WINKLE

This, too, has been deliberated upon. And again the Association is cordially willing that you pay it *yourselves.* Is that clear, sir?

SNODGRASS

Crystal clear, sir. And so in keeping with our precedents. I thank you.

(SNODGRASS *sits.*)

TUPMAN

Do I hear further remarks?

PICKWICK

Honorable Chairman . . .

TUPMAN

Mr. Pickwick . . .

(PICKWICK *rises. Applause. He holds up his hand for silence.*)

PICKWICK

Gentlemen, knowing we were likely to set forth on this journey, I have made a few small preparations. (*Draws a large telescope from his pocket*) With this instrument, gentlemen—with this miracle of modern science—we can better observe life. We can make small observations seem large and large observations seem small!

TUPMAN

Marvelous! May I see the instrument, sir?

PICKWICK

Certainly. (*He passes it around*) And in this—(*Takes a notebook from his pocket*) this notebook, and in *yours,* gentlemen, all can be faithfully recorded—*all*!

(*He passes out notebooks.*)

SNODGRASS

Notebooks! How practical!

WINKLE

How farsighted!

PICKWICK

Yet gentlemen, I must remind you that, although we have selected ourselves for a service of great honor, it also is one of some danger! (*Signs of apprehension from the Club*) This year of our Lord, 1827, is unprecedented in all history! If we are to believe the reports in our daily journals—and who can doubt them?—traveling is in a troubled state, and the minds of coachmen are unsettled!

WINKLE

True! True!

PICKWICK

Stagecoaches are upsetting in all directions! Horses are bolting on the public highways! Boats are overturning! Boilers are bursting! In short—the length and breadth of England—chaos reigns!

TUPMAN

(*Rising*)

But this will not deter us!

PICKWICK

Indeed not. In fact, to be intimate for a moment, nothing now stands in the way of our memorable journey but my landlady.

TUPMAN

(*Anxiously*)

Are you in trouble with your landlady, my dear Pickwick?

PICKWICK

Tupman, I am engaging a man-servant—one Samuel Weller. I fear Mrs. Bardell will think it a criticism of her housekeeping.

TUPMAN

And is it?

PICKWICK

Yes! I must approach the whole matter most tactfully. (*He rises*) Shall we go, dear friends?

(*The Club rises.*)

WINKLE

(*Rapping for attention*)

Gentlemen, before we adjourn, I beg to suggest that we surround, with a rich halo of enthusiastic approval, the name of our leader Mr. Samuel Pickwick.

THE CLUB

(*Led by* WINKLE)

Hip, hip, hooray! Hip, hip, hooray! Hip, hip, hooray!

PICKWICK

Gentlemen! Gentlemen, I am overcome. Let me shake you by the hand.

(*Hearty handshaking all around.*)

WINKLE

Well, my fellow-travelers. (*Takes bag*) To the task ahead!

SNODGRASS

(*Taking bag*)

To country paths and sylvan glens!

TUPMAN

(*Taking bag*)

And fair romance! Ah!

(PICKWICK *takes the last bag and starts for the door as* MRS. BARDELL *enters.*)

MRS. BARDELL

Have you forgotten the young man, sir?

PICKWICK

Indeed not. But I should like a word with you first, Mrs. Bardell. Kindly wait until I have deposited my luggage.

(PICKWICK *goes out.* MRS. BARDELL *crosses to the window as* MRS. CLUPPINS, *an acid-tongued old busybody, enters.*)

MRS. CLUPPINS

Just *why* is Mr. Pickwick leavin' you?

MRS. BARDELL

He's a-goin' off for a few weeks with some of the members of his Club.

MRS. CLUPPINS

(*Suspiciously*)

To do what?

MRS. BARDELL

To h'observe life, he said.

MRS. CLUPPINS

To h'observe life! You can do that right from this winder!

MRS. BARDELL

True. But Mr. Pickwick and his friends is eccentrics.

MRS. CLUPPINS

Ex what, dear?

MRS. BARDELL

Eccentrics. Leastwise that's what I heard several remark.

MRS. CLUPPINS

Well, I couldn't say as to that. I an't run acrost it.

MRS. BARDELL

Mr. Pickwick has led a sheltered life. Poor lamb, comin' into money from his father has affected him.

MRS. CLUPPINS

And now he jist wants to go on a spree. That's about it. Clubmen! All touched in the head . . . If they didn't have money, someone would say so straight out!

MRS. BARDELL

Well, touched or not, Mr. Pickwick has a partikler affectionate nature, I think.

MRS. CLUPPINS

Affectionate, you say?

MRS. BARDELL

(*Wistful*)

Affectionate.

MRS. CLUPPINS

All the same, he's leavin' you, an't he?

MRS. BARDELL

(*Sighing*)

Yes, and if ever I lets myself go, I could cry over it, Mrs. Cluppins.

MRS. CLUPPINS

Well, don't, dearie. It'll only swell your features and do nothin' to further the situation. Mrs. Bardell, you're a widder—and a good enough lookin' one at that.

MRS. BARDELL

Thank 'ee, dear.

MRS. CLUPPINS

(*Firm*)

But you ought to recognize that a man is a man—and one in your house is worth three in the street.

MRS. BARDELL

Oh la, Mrs. Cluppins! You *are* forward in your thoughts!

MRS. CLUPPINS

I'm speakin' from the heart! Has this Mr. Pickwick ever demonstrated his affection in any forceful way?

MRS. BARDELL

Well, he's called me a "good woman" on occasion.

MRS. CLUPPINS

(*Shaking her head*)

Tain't enough. Not near enough.

MRS. BARDELL

And once he said "dear Mrs. Bardell" . . .

MRS. CLUPPINS

That's a little more like it.

MRS. BARDELL

It may just have been impulsive-like. It was when he wanted a button sewed on his purty green waistcoat.

MRS. CLUPPINS

He don't sound too impulsive to me. Have you tried sidling up to him, lookin' into his eyes tender-like—brushin' a hand across his sleeve . . .

MRS. BARDELL

Dear me, no, Mrs. Cluppins!

MRS. CLUPPINS

Try it. Try it today. Partin' is a time of sorrow. Maybe he'll see you with new eyes, dearie. Who can tell?

MRS. BARDELL

(*Dreamily*)

Who indeed?

MRS. CLUPPINS

If there's one thing I'm sure on—you can't never read a man's thoughts. He may be a-standin' out there now buttonin' himself up—lookin' to all the world like he was just buttonin'—yet thinkin' on you all the time.

MRS. BARDELL

Oh, the sweet man! But I can't keep a lodger what wants to leave, can I?

MRS. CLUPPINS

If you puts your mind to it you can, dearie.

(MRS. CLUPPINS *goes.* MRS. BARDELL *stands dreaming a moment as* PICKWICK *enters.*)

PICKWICK

Now, Mrs. Bardell . . .

MRS. BARDELL

Yes, Mr. Pickwick?

PICKWICK

As you know, my friends and I are about to set out on a somewhat perilous journey. But before I go, there is something I want to ask you.

MRS. BARDELL

(*Fluttering*)

Anything! Anything you say, Mr. Pickwick!

PICKWICK

You have made me very comfortable here.

MRS. BARDELL

I have tried, sir. Yet there is more things I might have done —things only a woman can do for a man.

PICKWICK

Precisely. Just as there are things only a man can do.

MRS. BARDELL

True. True.

PICKWICK

Mrs. Bardell, do you think it a much greater expense to keep two people than to keep one?

MRS. BARDELL

La, Mr. Pickwick, what a question!

PICKWICK

Well, but *do* you?

MRS. BARDELL

Oh, that depends—that depends . . .

PICKWICK

Does it? On what?

MRS. BARDELL

Depends a great deal on the person, sir. And whether 'tis a saving and careful person, sir.

PICKWICK

Very true. But the person I have in my eye (*Looks very hard at* MRS. BARDELL) possesses these qualities, and has, moreover, a considerable knowledge of the world, which may be of great use to me.

MRS. BARDELL

(*More coquettish than ever*)

La, Mr. Pickwick! Go on, sir.

PICKWICK

To tell you the truth, Mrs. Bardell, I have made up my mind. You'll think it very strange I've never consulted you about this matter. It is only now, when I see my need . . .

MRS. BARDELL

Oh, you're very kind, sir!

PICKWICK

It'll save you a good deal of trouble, won't it?

MRS. BARDELL

Oh, but of course I should take more trouble to please you *then* than ever. It be kind of you, Mr. Pickwick, to have so much consideration for my loneliness.

PICKWICK

I never thought of that. When I return, you will always have somebody to sit with you.

MRS. BARDELL

I'm certain I ought to be a very happy woman.

PICKWICK

And your little boy . . .

MRS. BARDELL

Bless his innocent heart!

PICKWICK

He, too, will have a companion. A lively one who'll teach him, I'll be bound, more tricks in a week than he would ever learn in a year. Isn't that so?

MRS. BARDELL

(*Putting a hand on his arm*)

Oh, you dear—(PICKWICK, *startled, draws back*) Oh, you kind, good, playful, dear!

(*She flings her arms suddenly round his neck and breaks into a chorus of sobs.*)

PICKWICK

(*Astonished*)

Bless my soul! Mrs. Bardell, my good woman! Mrs. Bardell, *don't*! If anybody should come . . .

MRS. BARDELL

Oh, let them come! I'll never leave you, dear, kind, good, playful soul!

(*She clings tighter.*)

PICKWICK

Mercy on me! (*Struggles violently to free himself*) Don't! Don't! There's a good creature—HELP!

(*With a gasp* MRS. BARDELL *swoons in his arms, and before* PICKWICK *can deposit her on a chair,* TUPMAN, WINKLE *and* SNODGRASS *enter, stopping at the door in amazement. At the same time,* MRS. CLUPPINS *and* TOMMY *enter from the sitting-room. A pause, in which* PICKWICK *is speechless and unable to move.*)

TOMMY

(*Finally, rushing at* PICKWICK *and biting him*)

Leave Mama alone!

(*Bites* PICKWICK *on the leg*)

PICKWICK

Ouch! Ouch! Take the little villain away!

SNODGRASS

What *is* the matter, Pickwick?

PICKWICK

(*Pettishly*)

I don't know! Take away the boy! And—and—deposit this *woman* somewhere!

(*They all move to free him of* TOMMY *and to extract* MRS. BARDELL *from his arms.*)

MRS. BARDELL

(*Recovering*)

Oh! Oh! Where am I?

PICKWICK

Where, indeed!

TUPMAN

Do let me assist you, ma'am.

(*Takes her arm.*)

MRS. BARDELL

Thank 'ee, sir. Thank 'ee. Pray guide me to my sitting-room, sir.

TUPMAN

Gladly.

(TUPMAN *and* MRS. BARDELL *go.*)

MRS. CLUPPINS

(*At door, shaking a finger at* MR. PICKWICK)

Viper! Seducer!

(MRS. CLUPPINS *goes.* PICKWICK *stands bewildered, as they all stare hard at him.*)

PICKWICK

(*Finally*)

I—I cannot conceive what has been the matter with the woman. I was merely announcing to her my intention of engaging a man-servant when she fell into this—this *paroxysm* in which you found her. Very extraordinary thing.

SNODGRASS

Very.

PICKWICK

An extremely awkward situation.

WINKLE

Very.

SNODGRASS

(*Eyeing* PICKWICK)

Of course Mrs. Bardell *is* a most attractive widow.

WINKLE

Very.

PICKWICK

(*Bristling*)

Am I to believe, sirs, that you doubt my word?

SNODGRASS

Certainly not, sir.

TUPMAN

(*Re-entering*)

Pickwick, there's a man waiting for you outside.

PICKWICK

(*Curtly*)

Then have the goodness to call him in. We must be on our way and put this unfortunate experience behind us.

(SAM WELLER *enters.* SAM *is jaunty, likable, sure of himself. His clothes are disheveled and he wears a battered hat.*)

SAM

Vell, sir!

PICKWICK

Well, Sam! I'm very pleased to see you, my boy.

SAM

Me, too. And I hope our acquaintance may be a long 'un, as the gentleman said to the five-pound note!

(*They shake hands.*)

PICKWICK

Sam, these are my friends—Mr. Tupman, Mr. Winkle, and Mr. Snodgrass. If you become my man-servant, you'll see more of them. Mark them well.

SAM

(*Saluting them all*)

Salted in me memory, sir, as the gentleman said ven he pickled his seventh wife!

PICKWICK

Pickled his seventh wife! Dear me!

TUPMAN

What an extraordinary occurrence!

SAM

Not so h'extraordinary, when you thinks on the other six of 'em! (*To* PICKWICK) Well, sir, an't we got some talkin' to do?

SNODGRASS

Pickwick, would you rather we waited outside?

PICKWICK

Why?

WINKLE

You have such a—*private* life, dear Pickwick. Perhaps—your man-servant—who alone will share your secrets . . .

PICKWICK

(*With dignity*)

Winkle, my life is an open book. (*Then thoughtfully*) But, yes, wait outside. (SNODGRASS, WINKLE *and* TUPMAN *go out*) Now, Sam, with regard to the matter on which I sent for you . . .

SAM

That's the pint, sir! Out with it, as the father said to his child when he swallowed a shilling!

PICKWICK

(*Startled*)

You appear to be somewhat given to quotations.

SAM

True as true, sir.

PICKWICK

Time should prove whether this habit is a virtue or a vice. . . . Now, my man, have you any reason to be discontented with your present employment?

SAM

Afore I answers that 'ere question, sir, I should like to know whether you're a-goin' to purwide me with a better?

PICKWICK

I have half made up my mind to engage you.

SAM

(*Saucily*)

*Have* you, though? Servants is hard to come by these days. The question is, sir, is *my* mind half made up?

PICKWICK

Well, then, is it?

SAM

Wages?

PICKWICK

Twelve pounds a year.

SAM

Clothes?

PICKWICK

Two suits.

SAM

Work?

PICKWICK

To attend upon me and travel about with me and the gentlemen you just met.

SAM

Travel about where, sir?

PICKWICK

Wherever fate and fancy lead us.

SAM

H'mm. Sounds engagin'. Any wimmen to deal with?

PICKWICK

(*Startled*)

Women?

SAM

Wimmen.

PICKWICK

I'll have you know, Sam, that women play a very small part in my life. And I hope in yours.

SAM

(*Doubtfully*)

H'mm.

PICKWICK

You accept the position, then?

SAM

Take your sign down, sir! If the clothes fits me half as well as the activity, they'll do.

PICKWICK

The clothes? Ah, yes. (*Goes to closet, and pulls out a fantastic greatcoat with a large gilt P. C.* [*Pickwick Club*] *button on it, a black hat with a cockade, a pink striped waistcoat, very gay breeches, gaiters—in all, a noticeable livery*) There you are, my man! I'll wait you at the coach. So hurry!

(PICKWICK *goes out.*)

SAM

(*Holding up the fantastic livery, then staring into the mirror*) Well, it's a wonder! Am I meant to be a footman, a groom, a gamekeeper or a strollin' actor? I looks like sort of a puddin' of 'em all. Well, never mind. Mr. Pickwick an't like no other gentlemen, and neither am I. On that account, we wuz drawn to each other. So, long life to the Pickvicks, says I!

PICKWICK

(*Off stage, calling*)

Sam! Sam!

SAM

(*Grabbing his bundle of new clothes, clapping his hat on*)

Comin', sir! Comin' *fast*—as the feller said ven his foot slipped on the mountain side!

(*He hurries off as* MRS. CLUPPINS *and* MRS. BARDELL *re-enter.* MRS. CLUPPINS *is bending over* MRS. BARDELL *and trying to comfort the tearful woman.*)

MRS. CLUPPINS

There now, dearie, don't let it decompose you! Men is all alike. They says one thing today, another tomorrow. Took me seven years to get Mr. Cluppins to the h'altar.

MRS. BARDELL

Seven years! Oh, dear!

(*Sobs again.*)

MRS. CLUPPINS

And this Mr. Pickwick—he's a more slippery one than Cluppie, I'll warrant. But don't fret. He'll pay for it!

MRS. BARDELL

Pay for it?

MRS. CLUPPINS

He will that! I sent Tommy for the solicitor.

MRS. BARDELL

The solicitor? Dear me, why?

MRS. CLUPPINS

Because the law's the law! And in the sight of the court your affections has been trifled with!

MRS. BARDELL

(*Weakly*)

Have they?

MRS. CLUPPINS

Indeed they have.

MRS. BARDELL

Oh, but I don't want to embroil Mr. Pickwick with the law!

MRS. CLUPPINS

(*Firmly*)

Yes, you do, dearie.

MRS. BARDELL

But you should have heard him, Mrs. Cluppins. So tender he was, and playful.

MRS. CLUPPINS

I did hear a bit of it.

MRS. BARDELL

(*Looking up, dry-eyed*)

You listened? That's shameful, Mrs. Cluppins.

MRS. CLUPPINS

'Tis one woman's duty to protect another. Of the sexes, an't we the weaker?

MRS. BARDELL

What a pity to have my sorrow known to all!

MRS. CLUPPINS

Your secret is safe with me, dear. I an't a meddler and never wuz.

(*At this moment* TOMMY *bursts into the room followed by a large pompous man dressed in a black coat, striped trousers and black gaiters. He is* MR. SERJEANT BUZFUZ.)

TOMMY

(*Triumphantly*)

Here he is! I got him!

MRS. CLUPPINS

(*To* MRS. BARDELL)

Dry your eyes, dear. The solicitor's come.

SERJEANT BUZFUZ

(*Very formal*)

I am Mr. Serjeant Buzfuz of Dodson and Fogg, Solicitors. What are the circumstances which require my service?

MRS. CLUPPINS

Tell the gentleman, dear.

MRS. BARDELL

(*Timidly*)

Oh, oh, I hardly know what to say on it, sir.

BUZFUZ

Come, ma'am. State the facts. Great ones for the facts, Dodson and Fogg. Particularly Fogg.

(*Takes out his notebook.*)

MRS. CLUPPINS

Go on, dearie, speak up.

MRS. BARDELL

Well, he—he proposed . . .

BUZFUZ

Proposed what, ma'am?

MRS. CLUPPINS

A bald-faced offer of seduction—clothed in matrimony!

BUZFUZ

Ah! And who took this forward step?

MRS. CLUPPINS

Her lodger it wuz—Mr. Pickwick.

BUZFUZ

And then what, ma'am?

MRS. BARDELL

(*Sobbing again*)

Oh, I—the dear man! Must I tell?

BUZFUZ

Do not allow your feelings to overcome you, ma'am. If an injury has been done you, retribution is called for.

MRS. CLUPPINS

My very words!

MRS. BARDELL

Oh, I don't want to trouble him! *I* don't!

BUZFUZ

No trouble at all, ma'am, providing the case interests me. Mrs. Cluppins, state briefly what you know of this Mr. Pickwick.

MRS. CLUPPINS

He's a single gentleman of means. A reg'lar bloomin' swell. He's got a fortune!

BUZFUZ

The case interests me . . . Now, ma'am, state the injury suffered.

MRS. CLUPPINS

He proposed, was found in an uncompromisin' position, and denied everything.

BUZFUZ

Ha! A breach of promise, eh?

MRS. BARDELL

A what?

BUZFUZ

Where is the gentleman in question?

MRS. BARDELL

Gone.

BUZFUZ

Where?

MRS. BARDELL

(*Wailing again*)

Oh, I don't know. I don't know!

TOMMY

*I* know—to Chatham.

(BUZFUZ *makes a note.*)

BUZFUZ

Trying to flee the consequences, eh? Ma'am, you will hear from me.

MRS. BARDELL

(*Anxiously*)

What are you going to do, sir?

BUZFUZ

Sue him, ma'am. Make him pay for meddling with your maidenly feelings. Mrs. Cluppins, you will act as witness?

MRS. CLUPPINS

(*Pleased*)

Thank 'ee, sir.

BUZFUZ

Excellent. The firm of Dodson and Fogg will do the rest. Never a case too small where justice is involved. (*Turns to* MRS. CLUPPINS) How much a year did you say this Pickwick has?

MRS. CLUPPINS

Mrs. Bardell, dear, tell the gentleman how much income Mr. Pickwick has.

MRS. BARDELL

Oh, I—I couldn't say rightly. A great deal, I s'pose. Thousands! But you won't . . .

BUZFUZ

(*Brightening, as he comes over and takes her hand*)

Grieve no longer, ma'am. The strong arm of the law will protect you from this monstrous assault upon your womanly innocence!

(*He goes out.*)

MRS. CLUPPINS

(*Looking after him dreamily*)

Don't he speak it jist bewtiful!

*THE CURTAIN FALLS*

# ACT 1

## SCENE II

*SCENE: The main room of the Town Arms Inn, Chatham. The entrance is on the right. A door, left, leads to the kitchen; stairs, rear, to the bedrooms. There is a window alcove, rear, which affords a certain privacy from the tables in the main room.*

*Large posters are hung at the windows: "VOTE FOR SLUMKEY" "VOTE FOR FIZKIN" "DOWN WITH SLUMKEY" "DOWN WITH FIZKIN."*

*AT RISE: A large florid man,* MR. WELLER, *father of* SAM, *and his wife, an equally high-colored but more energetic female, are looking out the window. There is considerable noise and general commotion in the street outside, and occasional cheering. The crowd and activities can be seen through the window, rear.*

*The only other occupant of the Inn is* MR. STIGGINS, *a thin-faced, red-nosed cleric seated to one side at a table drinking grog. He seems disinterested in the excitement outside.*

MRS. WELLER

(*Leaning out the window*)

There's Mr. Slumkey! He's a-showin' hisself to the crowd!

(*Cheers outside.*)

MR. WELLER

He'd likely get more votes if he omitted that 'ere performance.

MRS. WELLER

He has shook hands with the men! (*Another cheer*) He has patted the babies on the head! (*A louder cheer*) He has kissed one of 'em! He has kissed another! (*A still louder cheer*) He has kissed 'em all!

(*A roar outside.*)

MR. WELLER

He'll be too blessed weak to hold office.

MR. STIGGINS

(*Drunkenly, to himself*)

Vanity. All ish vanity.

(WELLER *glances with distaste at* STIGGINS.)

WELLER

(*To* MRS. WELLER)

Don't your friend, the shepherd, approve of Election Day?

MRS. WELLER

Ssh! Mr. Stiggins is thinkin'. Crowds allays makes him thoughtful!

WELLER

Well, for a temperance man, he needs a deal of primin'. Costs you and me nigh on to three bottles a thought.

MRS. WELLER

His words are inspired! They lift us all!

WELLER

They don't lift me, my love.

MRS. WELLER

You jist ain't spiritual, Mr. Weller. I thought you wuz when I married you, but it's been proved different.

WELLER

Ditto, my love. Ditto. (*Looks out of window again, then turns back eagerly*) Well, I'll be bound, there's Sam! Dressed up like a circus man and attendin' on some fine gentlemen!

MRS. WELLER

Not comin' here, is he? I wuz in hopes we'd never see that young jackanapes again.

WELLER

You're speakin' of my own flesh and blood, ma'am. Five years since I've seen Samivel. Turned him out of house and home, I did. Wanted to give him a start in life, as the man said when he tickled the horse with a feather.

STIGGINS

(*Calling over*)

A little more warm water and sugar, if you please, ma'am.

WELLER

(*With sarcasm*)

What! No more rum? The man's bilious.

MRS. WELLER

Come with me, Mr. Stiggins. I'll make something jist proper for you in the kitchen.

(STIGGINS *gets up unsteadily and starts for the kitchen.*)

WELLER

It's a great pleasure to see you able to walk so late in the day, Mr. Stiggins.

STIGGINS

(*Turning*)

Everyone misunderstands me because I'm executing the Lord's work.

WELLER

Is *that* what you're a-doin'? It's a fair wonder to me salvation don't hit more people.

(STIGGINS *goes out.*)

MRS. WELLER

(*At the door*)

Remember, we've got no rooms for that son of yours. Nor fer his friends, neither.

WELLER

Am I master of my own Inn, my love? Am I or an't I?

MRS. WELLER

(*Flatly*)

You an't!

(MRS. WELLER *goes out, just as* SAM, *dressed in the fantastic clothes* PICKWICK *has given him, enters with luggage.*)

SAM

(*Advancing toward his father*)

Well, if it's not the old un!

WELLER

(*Warmly*)

Sammy! Come to my arms!

(*They embrace.*)

SAM

How are you, my ancient!

WELLER

Greatly changed. Greatly changed. And so be you, little one.

SAM

You're not a day older, old codger. How's stepmother?

WELLER

(*Solemnly, in a low voice*)

Vy, I'll tell you what, Sammy—as a widder there never was a nicer woman than this 'ere second wenture o' mine—a sweet creetur she was, Samivel—but, well, all I can say on her now—she was such an uncommon pleasant widder, it's a great pity she ever changed her condition!

SAM

What's the trouble with her, old 'un?

WELLER

Well, Samivel, either she don't act like a wife, or she acts too much like one. The woman's got no between. (*Shakes his head and sighs*) Also—she's gettin' rather of the theological persuasion lately. Spends her life at meetings a-tea drinkin' with fourteen women and a feller they calls the Deputy Shepherd—with a red nose.

SAM

A red nose?

WELLER

That's it. A very red-nosed feller.

SAM

So's his flock can see him the better?

WELLER

Can't say as to that, Samivel—but when at the tea-drinkin' the Deputy Shepherd says "the kiss of peace" and kisses 'em all around, my stummick jist plain rebels!

SAM

All this is done on tea?

WELLER

Ah, but the tea's for the women only. This 'ere Shepherd—when he sees a bottle he never leaves nothin' in it but the cork and the smell . . . And that's what I'm up against, Sammy. Queer, my boy, queer. I'm blest if some day I don't jist up and go away to Ameriker!

SAM

Ain't that purty desperate, old codger?

WELLER

These is desperate times, Samivel.

SAM

Well, from what I hears, even the 'Merrikins is addicted to matrimony.

WELLER

But there's some space in that 'ere country to get away from it! No, I've done this matrimony once too often, Sammy. Take example of your father, my boy, and be careful, especially of widders—more especially of widders that keeps taverns. Marriage is a bewtiful picture—till it's painted. If ever you feels disposed to go a-marryin' anybody, Sammy, jist you shut yourself up in your room, if you has one, and pison yourself off-hand. You'll be glad on it arterwards. (*Looks at him sharply*) You wudn't be already attached, wud you?

SAM

No, guv'nor. I'm without a mate, as the sea captain remarked ven the wave washed over the ship!

WELLER

(*Chuckling*)

That's a good 'un, Samivel! Did I ever say that one?

SAM

Don't believe you did, guv'nor.

WELLER

By the bye, that rig, Sammy. Are you well paid for wearing it?

SAM

I am. I'm in service to a gentleman.

MR. WELLER

Doin' what?

SAM

H'observin' life.

MR. WELLER

Sounds interestin'—if you has the time for it!

SAM

'Tis interestin'—only the gentleman and his friends is all so h'observin', the *work* falls to me! Which brings me to my point —can you lodge us, guv'nor? Party of four and me?

WELLER

H'mm. Ever' bed's got a foot in it tonight, Sammy. But o' course, it bein' Election Day, there's bound to be some that won't know the bed from the floor by midnight. (*Takes his arm*) Come along, my urchin. I'll uncover a nesting-place for you, seein' as yer my own flesh and blood.

(*They go out. Through the large window, rear, the election crowd can be seen again, and cheering starts up. Suddenly* WINKLE *appears outside, waving his arms violently to someone in the distance. Immediately we see him struck by a bystander, then another man rushes to his rescue. A moment later, a tall, haggard, seedy-looking individual enters the tavern, followed by* WINKLE *who holds one hand over his eye, and clutches his fieldpiece in his other hand. The seedy-looking individual is* ALFRED JINGLE, ESQUIRE, *a man of jaunty impudence and singular self-possession.*)

JINGLE

(*Calling loudly*)

I say, barmaid! Keeper! (JINGLE *guides* WINKLE *to a chair. It is evident that* WINKLE *has a very black eye*) Spirited election, eh, sir? Accidents will happen—best-regulated families—never say die—down on your luck—pull yourself up, eh—damned rascals! How's your eye? No matter. Stare 'em down!

WINKLE

(*Petulantly*)

But whyever did they strike me? I didn't say whether I was for Slumkey or Fizkin!

JINGLE

No matter, sir. Two mobs—always yell with the loudest! Ha! Ha! (MRS. WELLER *appears*) Here, ma'am! Glasses around—brandy and water—hot and strong—sweet and plenty!

MRS. WELLER

How many, sir?

JINGLE

(*To* WINKLE)

Many friends, sir? (WINKLE *does not answer*) Safe to bring five glasses. Beefsteak, too! Make it raw! Eye damaged here. Bad bruise. Ailing gentleman—hurry! (MRS. WELLER *takes a look at* WINKLE *and goes out*) For black eye—cold lamppost good as beefsteak—but lamppost inconvenient—damned odd standing in open street half an hour, eye against a lamppost—eh?—very good—ha! ha!

(SNODGRASS, PICKWICK *and* TUPMAN *enter hurriedly, notebooks in hand. They all wear, along with* WINKLE, *vivid green coats with a large gilt* "P.C." *button.* JINGLE *waves them over.*)

Here, gentlemen!

PICKWICK

(*Hurrying over, anxiously*)

How are you, Winkle? The man was mad to attack you!

SNODGRASS

But we took full notes on the whole affair!

WINKLE

Good. I should hate to have this pass unrecorded.

PICKWICK

(*To* JINGLE)

I do thank you for your timely rescue of my friend, Mr.— Mr.—

JINGLE

Jingle, sir. Alfred Jingle, Esquire. Glad to be of service—always court danger—happened along.

PICKWICK

You were just in time, sir!

JINGLE

Fate, sir. Fate. Other day—riding on a coach—low archway in front—"heads, head," I said, "take care of your heads!" Five children, mother on top—tall lady eating sandwiches—forgot the arch—crash—knock—children look round—mother's head off—sandwich in her hand—no mouth to put it in—head of a family off—shocking, shocking! Eh, sir?

PICKWICK

(*Staring*)

Very. (*Turns to* WINKLE, *who is rubbing his eye*) Is it painful, Winkle?

WINKLE

It is a wound to my dignity, Pickwick.

PICKWICK

Dear, dear. Most unfortunate.

(MRS. WELLER *enters with drinks and the beefsteak.* JINGLE *takes beefsteak and claps it to* WINKLE'S *eye.*)

JINGLE

Ah! The beefsteak. Capital, eh? Meat to the eye. Well met, eh?

MRS. WELLER

Who's payin'?

JINGLE

(*Quickly, to* PICKWICK)

Brandy to you, sir? Not worth while splitting a guinea, eh? (PICKWICK *pays.* MRS. WELLER *goes out.* PICKWICK *sits silently.* WINKLE *holds the beefsteak to his eye. The others also are silent. Then, very heartily*) Well, sirs! Well, sirs! Excellent brandy—flow of talk—gloom banished—Anything wrong?

PICKWICK

I was ruminating, sir, on these strange accidents and the unexpectedness of human affairs.

JINGLE

Philosopher, sir?

PICKWICK

An observer of human nature, sir.

JINGLE

Ah, capital! So am I. Most people are when they've little to do and less to get. Poet, also, sir?

PICKWICK

My friend Mr. Snodgrass has a strong poetic turn.

JINGLE

(*Quickly, to* SNODGRASS)

So have I. Epic poem—ten thousand lines—revolution of July—composed it on the spot—Mars by day, Apollo by night—bang the fieldpiece, twang the lyre—noble time, sir. (*Turns abruptly to* WINKLE) Sportsman, sir?

WINKLE

A little, sir, as you see.
(*Holds up the fieldpiece.*)

JINGLE

Fine pursuit, sir—fine pursuit. Dogs, sir?

WINKLE

Not just now.

JINGLE

(*Quickly*)

Ah! Should keep dogs—fine animals—sagacious creatures—dog of my own once—pointer—surprising instinct—out shooting one day—entering enclosure—whistled—dog stopped—whistled again—Ponto—Ponto—no go; stock still—called him—Ponto—Ponto—wouldn't move—dog transfixed—staring at board—looked up, saw inscription—"Gamekeeper has orders to shoot all dogs found in his enclosure"—wouldn't pass it—wonderful dog that—valuable—very.

PICKWICK

(*Pulling out his notebook*)

What a singular circumstance, sir. Will you allow me to make a note of it?

JINGLE

Certainly, sir, certainly—hundred more anecdotes same animal, if you like. (PICKWICK *starts writing. At this moment a pretty young girl,* MARY, *dressed as a maid-servant, enters the*

*Inn and passes by the table and on out into the kitchen.* JINGLE *turns quickly to* TUPMAN) Fine girl, eh, sir?

TUPMAN

Very.

JINGLE

English girls not so fine as Spanish, though—noble creatures—jet hair—black eyes—lovely forms—sweet creatures—beautiful.

TUPMAN

You have been in Spain, sir?

JINGLE

Lived there—ages.

TUPMAN

Many conquests, sir?

JINGLE

Conquests? Thousands! Don Bolaro Fizzgig—grandee—only daughter—Donna Christina—splendid creature—loved me to distraction—jealous father—high-souled daughter—handsome Englishman—Donna Christina in despair—prussic acid—stomach pump in my portmanteau—operation performed—old Bolaro in ecstasies—consent to our union—join hands—floods of tears—romantic story—very.

TUPMAN

Is the lady in England now, sir?

JINGLE

Dead, sir—dead. (*Wipes his eyes briefly with his handkerchief*) Never recovered stomach pump—undermined constitution—fell a victim.

SNODGRASS

And her father?

JINGLE

Sudden disappearance—talk of the whole city—search made everywhere—public fountain in square—suddenly ceased playing—weeks elapsed—still a stoppage—workmen employed—water drawn off—father-in-law discovered sticking head-first in main pipe—full confession in his right boot—took him out—fountain played again—well as ever.

PICKWICK

(*Taking out notebook*)

Will you allow me to note that little romance down, sir?

JINGLE

Certainly, sir, certainly. Fifty more if you'd like to hear 'em—strange life, mine—rather curious history—not extraordinary, but singular.

(*Gulps his brandy down.*)

PICKWICK

(*To* JINGLE)

Sir, you rendered us a very important service this morning. May we beg the favor of your company at dinner?

JINGLE

(*With alacrity*)

Great pleasure. Break other engagements. New friends. New thoughts. (*Lowers voice*) Not presume to dictate, but broiled fowl and mushroom here—capital—what time?

PICKWICK

(*Consulting his friends*)

Shall we say five?

ALL

Five.

JINGLE

Excellent! Five precisely. Till then—care of yourselves! (*He moves toward the door just as* MR. STIGGINS, *who hugs a bottle under his arm, enters.*) Ah, Mr. Stiggins. Allow me to help, sir. (*Takes bottle, then* STIGGINS' *arm*) Full bottle. Lonely soul. Miserable. Sit down together. Raise glass. Friends for life! Come, sir!

(JINGLE *steers out the reluctant* MR. STIGGINS.)

TUPMAN

Evidently a traveler in many countries, and a close observer of men and things.

SNODGRASS

Could have been a poet.

WINKLE

I should like to have seen that dog.

(*They all stare ahead thoughtfully.* SAM *enters and stands a moment watching them.*)

SAM

Well, gentlemen, whatever be you h'observin' on now?

PICKWICK

(*Without looking up*)

Life is very full, Sam. Did you find quarters?

SAM

Quarters not to be had, sir—but I got 'em anyway. Interestin' rascal, my father!

PICKWICK

(*Startled*)

Rascal, Sam?

SAM

Could ha' been a regular politician himself—if he'd had the h'energy. Out there now with two fellers—pumping water over the heads of the independent voters—a shilling a head, if they gets 'em sober and ready to vote the proper way!

PICKWICK

Mercy! Can such things be?

SAM

Take a look at the pump, sir. They're workin' it hard.

(PICKWICK *and the others cross and look out.*)

PICKWICK

Shocking!

TUPMAN

Disgraceful!

SAM

Bless your hearts, sir—that's nothin'! Stepmother's out there this minute hocussin' the brandy and water for fourteen voters of the h'opposite party.

PICKWICK

What do you mean, Sam—"hocussing" the brandy and water?

SAM

Puttin' a drop of somethin' in it that'll send 'em all to sleep till twelve hours after the election.

PICKWICK

What extraordinary practices! Gentlemen, we must note them down.

(*They all return to their seats and write solemnly.*)

SAM

Could I ask a question, sir?

PICKWICK

(*Without looking up*)

Proceed.

SAM

Did you h'observe on a young female who walked through here a few minutes back?

PICKWICK

I have no direct memory of any young female, Sam.

TUPMAN

I caught a glimpse of her, Sam. A young Englishwoman, I believe.

SAM

That all?

TUPMAN

A *pretty* one, I believe.

SAM

Ah! That's more like a genuine h'observation! Turns out to be named Mary and, to get to the point, she's free for the evenin', sir.

PICKWICK

Are you suggesting that you take the evening off, Sam?

SAM

I was merely h'observin' that opportunity is opportunity and this bein' Election Day, *some* masters . . .

PICKWICK

Say no more, Sam. Look after the luggage. And the evening is yours.

SAM

Thank 'ee, sir.

PICKWICK

I trust, however, this—adventure—will lead to no—er—permanent connections.

SAM

I'm a-hopin' the same, sir—though at this partikler junction I can promise nothing, sir.

(*At this moment* MARY *enters and crosses the room.* SAM *takes off after her, and out.*)

SNODGRASS

(*Looking up from his notebook*)

Gentlemen, am I right in thinking we have been to the towns of Stroud, Rochester, Brompton and Chatham?

PICKWICK

You are, sir.

SNODGRASS

What think you of this quatrain?

"Stroud, Rochester, Brompton and Chatham,
We have been in 'em and we have been at 'em,
And all we've seen is here verbatim
Of Stroud, Rochester, Brompton and Chatham!"

Of course, that is not the final form.

PICKWICK

Of course not.

SNODGRASS

(*Annoyed*)

What do you mean, sir?

(SAM *re-enters, bearing a card.*)

SAM

Pardon, sir. Person wants you partikler, sir—and no one else'll do, as the devil's private secretary said ven he fetched away Dr. Faustus. (*Holds out card*) Here's her label.

PICKWICK

(*Examining card*)

A lady, Sam?

SAM

Well, a very good imitation o' one, if it an't. Says she'll wait all day raythe than not set eyes on you.

TUPMAN

Can a lady be so bold?

PICKWICK

It must be a matter of great urgency. Send her in, Sam.

(SAM *goes out.* PICKWICK *stands reflectively, studying the card. At this moment, a rangy and determined-looking female of fifty sweeps in from the outside and advances with outstretched hand. She is* MRS. LEO HUNTER.)

MRS. HUNTER

Mr. Pickwick, I presume? (PICKWICK *bows*) Allow me, sir, the honor of grasping your hand. Permit me, sir, to shake it. (*She shakes hand forcefully.* PICKWICK *winces*) I have heard of your fame, sir. The noise of your new scientific club and its observations has reached my ears, sir. I am Mrs. Leo Wilburforce Hunter.

PICKWICK

Madam, my friends—Mr. Winkle, Mr. Tupman, Mr. Snodgrass.

(*She shakes hands with all of them.*)

MRS. HUNTER

Gentlemen, I am proud to number among my acquaintances all those celebrated by their works and talents. Permit me, sir, to place in a conspicuous part of the list the name of Mr. Pickwick, and his brother members of the Club that derives its name from him.

PICKWICK

Very flattering, ma'am.

MRS. HUNTER

Tomorrow, sir, I am giving a public breakfast—a fête champêtre. Permit me, sir, to have the gratification of seeing you at the—Delphic Den.

WINKLE

(*Doubtfully*)

The Delphic Den?

MRS. HUNTER

The Delphic Den. The name of my little place, sir.

WINKLE

Very pretty.

MRS. HUNTER

I have many of these public occasions, sir—"feasts of reason," sir, and "flows of soul," as somebody who wrote a sonnet to my breakfasts feelingly and originally observed.

PICKWICK

Was *he* celebrated for his works and talents?

MRS. HUNTER

He was, sir. All of my acquaintances are. It is my ambition, sir, to have no other acquaintances.

PICKWICK

It is a very noble ambition.

MRS. HUNTER

(*Pleased*)

When I hear *that* remark fall from *your* lips, sir, I am indeed proud. You have a gentleman in your party who has produced some poems, sir?

PICKWICK

My friend, Mr. Snodgrass, has a great taste for poetry.

MRS. HUNTER

So have I, sir. I dote on poetry, sir! I adore it! I may say that my whole soul and mind are wound up and entwined with it! I have produced some pieces myself, sir.

SNODGRASS

(*Stiffly*)

Indeed?

MRS. HUNTER

You have met, sir, with my "Ode to an Expiring Frog"?

SNODGRASS

If I have, ma'am, I do not recall the occasion.

MRS. HUNTER

You astonish me, sir. It created an immense sensation when it appeared originally in the *Sylvan Echo* . . .

PICKWICK

Indeed? We have not been privileged to see the—*Sylvan Echo,* ma'am—but I—I should like to hear your poem.

(*They* ALL *murmur assent except* SNODGRASS, *who turns away haughtily.*)

MRS. HUNTER

Oh, you *shall,* gentlemen, you shall! I am reciting it, in character—at my breakfast party.

PICKWICK

In character!

MRS. HUNTER

As Minerva. I neglected to explain, sirs, it will be a fancy-dress breakfast.

PICKWICK

(*Dismayed*)

Dear me! But we have only these simple club garments. I do fear we can't possibly . . .

MRS. HUNTER

Can't, sir! Can't! Solomon Lucas, in High Street, has thousands of fancy dresses for hire.

PICKWICK

We shall need only four, ma'am.

MRS. HUNTER

Consider how many, many appropriate characters are open to your selection. Plato, Zeno, Epicurus, Pythagoras—all founders of clubs!

PICKWICK

But my dear Mrs. Hunter, we cannot put ourselves in competition with those great men. We could never presume to wear their attire.

(*They all assent modestly. A pause.*)

MRS. HUNTER

(*Gravely*)

On reflection, sirs, I doubt if it would not afford me even greater pleasure if gentlemen of your celebrity came in your *own* costumes. (*The faces of the* PICKWICKIANS *brighten*) Yes, I may venture to promise an exception in your case, sirs—yes, I may so venture.

PICKWICK

(*Relieved*)

In that case, we shall have the greatest pleasure in coming.

MRS. HUNTER

Excellent!

PICKWICK

If Fate does not intervene, ma'am.

MRS. HUNTER

Ah Fate! Fate! (*She rises abruptly*) I will not detain you further. (*She seizes* PICKWICK *and the others by the hands and shakes them vigorously*) Good afternoon, gentlemen. Good afternoon. I am proud to have beheld such eminent personages. (*She heads for the door.* PICKWICK *steps forward but* MRS. HUNTER *stops him with a gesture*) Not a step, sir! Not a step! Your time—far too dear!

(MRS. HUNTER *whirls out.*)

PICKWICK

(*Staring after her*)

What a remarkable female!

WINKLE

Very.

TUPMAN

Most stimulating! I think, after all, I *shall* go to her breakfast party in fancy dress. (*They all stare at* TUPMAN) Yes! I know just the thing. I shall go as a bandit.

PICKWICK

(*Shocked*)

What!

TUPMAN

Yes, as a bandit.

PICKWICK

(*Amicably critical*)

You don't mean to say, sir, that it is your intention to put yourself into a green velvet jacket, with a two-inch tail?

TUPMAN

(*Bristling*)

Such *was* my intention, sir. And why not, sir?

PICKWICK

Because, sir—because you are too old, sir.

TUPMAN

Too old!

PICKWICK

And if any further ground of objection be wanting, you are too fat, sir.

TUPMAN

Sir, that is an insult!

PICKWICK

Sir, it is not half the insult to *you* that *your* appearance in my presence in a green velvet jacket, with a two-inch tail, would be to me.

TUPMAN

(*Rising*)

Sir, you are—a—a *fellow*!

PICKWICK

(*Rising*)

Sir! You're another!

TUPMAN

You have called me old!

PICKWICK

I have!

TUPMAN

And fat!

PICKWICK

I reiterate the charge!

TUPMAN

And a—a fellow!

PICKWICK

So you are!

(*A fearful pause.*)

TUPMAN

My attachment to your person, sir, is great—very great—but upon that person I must take summary vengeance!

(TUPMAN *peels off his coat;* PICKWICK *does the same.*)

PICKWICK

(*Placing himself in an awkward attitude he believes to be defensive*)

Very well. Come on, sir!

(*Another fearful pause.*)

SNODGRASS

(*Jumping between them*)

Gentlemen! "Consider Passion!"

WINKLE

"Look before you Leap!"

(PICKWICK *and* TUPMAN *still stand squared off. A long pause in which the stern countenance of* PICKWICK *melts back to its usual benignity.*)

PICKWICK

Tupman, I have been hasty. Your hand, sir.

TUPMAN

I have been hasty, too. (*They grasp hands*) You, sir, go as the bandit in my stead.

PICKWICK

Never, never! Dear friend, I am humbled by this outbreak of passion. I trust the beast will never rise in my bosom again.

TUPMAN

I, too.

*(They put their coats on again. At this moment,* MR. WARDLE, *a jolly-looking country squire, and three women enter:* RACHEL WARDLE, *an equine-faced spinster, and the* MISSES EMILY *and* ISABELLA, *rather attractive young girls.* WARDLE'S *servant,* JOE, *a very sleepy fat boy, follows them in and, after depositing the luggage, promptly sits on it and dozes.)*

WARDLE

Ah! Many guests. Good. (*Advancing cordially*) Why, Mr. Pickwick! Heard you were here. Delighted to see you.

PICKWICK

Bless my soul! Wardle. Welcome! You know my friends, of course?

WARDLE

Certainly. Know 'em well! (WARDLE *shakes hands all round, then turns to* JOE) Joe! Damn that boy—gone to sleep again! (*Goes over, shakes* JOE) Joe—bring in the boxes. Quick about it! (JOE *rouses himself slowly and goes out.* WARDLE *ushers the two young women forward*) These are my daughters, gentlemen—Isabella and Emily. (ISABELLA *and* EMILY *cross and bow to all the Pickwickians*) And my sister, Miss Rachel Wardle. (PICKWICK *bows to* MISS RACHEL. JOE, SAM *and* MARY—*the pretty girl who caught* SAM'S *attention earlier—enter with suitcases, portmanteaus, baskets, etc.*) Always come in for Election Day. Much excitement. Much to eat and drink. Don't care a farthing for it myself—but the girls here, must see life, you know. Ha!

(JOE, SAM *and* MARY *go out*—SAM *appraising* MARY *with his eyes.*)

PICKWICK

(*To* MRS. WELLER, *who has entered*)

A bowl of punch—and brandy for the gentlemen. Will you have a glass of brandy?

WARDLE

With the greatest of pleasure.

(*They move to the tables and are just being seated when* JINGLE *enters and comes over breezily.*)

JINGLE

Well, merry party! Pretty girls! Glorious day! (*Looks at watch*) Five to the dot. When's dinner?

PICKWICK

Mr. Wardle—and ladies—a friend of mine, Mr. Jingle.

JINGLE

(*Bowing, then grasping* WARDLE's *hand with fervor*)

Ladies. Friend of yours! My dear sir, how are you? Friend of *my* friend's—give me your hand, sir . . .

(WARDLE *stiffens visibly before this enthusiasm and breaks away.*)

WARDLE

I might as well admit, Pickwick, my sister Rachel wanted particularly to see you. She is also a scientist. A naturalist, you know! That sort of thing. She observes moths.

PICKWICK

Moths?

WARDLE

Yes, moths.

RACHEL

Only *day* moths, brother dear.

WARDLE

Quite. Never out at night, my sister.

PICKWICK

A *lady* interested in science! How noteworthy! I've never met a lady with such strong pursuits.

WARDLE

Well, she can afford it. Got her own income, you know.

(JINGLE, *hearing these words, positively leaps around to* RACHEL.)

JINGLE

Used to keep moths myself, ma'am. South Africa—wonderful specimens—trunk filled with 'em.

RACHEL

Indeed, sir?

WARDLE

(*Interrupting quickly*)

Speaking of moths, we just came from the cricket match. Did you see it?

JINGLE

Noble game—well played—some strokes admirable.

WARDLE

You have played it, sir?

JINGLE

Played it! Think I have—thousands of times—not here—West Indies—exciting thing—hot work—very.

WARDLE

(*Regarding* JINGLE *dubiously*)

It seems to me I've seen you before, sir.

JINGLE

Very possibly, sir.

WARDLE

(*Accusingly*)

It was on the stage, sir! You were standing on your head, surrounded by fireworks!

JINGLE

(*Drawing him aside, quickly*)

Oh! Younger brother, sir—interested in the arts—good actor—well connected—not desirous of having it generally known—footlights alluring—sink or swim—starve or live as fortune wills . . .

(MRS. WELLER *enters with punch and brandy.*)

WARDLE

(*Drawing away from* JINGLE *with distaste*)

If you will excuse me, sir—I'll hear of it later. We must get settled before dinner. Roads very dusty. Come, my dears.

(*Gulps down his brandy.*)

PICKWICK

(*Looking at* RACHEL)

I trust we may all have dinner together.

JINGLE

More the merrier. Don't you think? Ha! Ha!

WARDLE

(*To* PICKWICK)

With pleasure.

(WARDLE *and the young women move off.*)

JINGLE

Must find innkeeper. Fowls, pies, wines—know just the thing!

(*He goes off, taking* WINKLE, TUPMAN *and* SNODGRASS *with him.* RACHEL *is near the door when* PICKWICK *calls her.*)

PICKWICK

Miss Wardle . . .

RACHEL

(*Turning*)

Mr. Pickwick?

PICKWICK

I am so taken by the thought of your moths, I should like the opportunity to record your observations.

RACHEL

Would you, sir?

PICKWICK

I hope we shall be able to snatch some moments alone during your stay.

RACHEL

Alone! Oh, sir, you *are* bold.

(*She moves to go.*)

PICKWICK

(*Alarmed*)

Stop. I meant no offense, ma'am.

RACHEL

Oh, I was not offended, sir.

PICKWICK

May I see you to the stairs, then?

RACHEL

Do, sir. Do.

(JINGLE *re-enters from the kitchen rubbing his hands with enthusiasm.*)

JINGLE

Ah—capital dinner! Ordered! All under way, Pickwick! But needs your eye, my man! (*Urges* PICKWICK *toward kitchen, grabs* RACHEL's *arm*) Escort you to your rooms, ma'am? Blackguards in the halls—confusion—single lady—charming—alone in world—needs protection!

(JINGLE *sweeps up the stairs with* RACHEL. PICKWICK, *bewildered by this swift action, follows them a few paces up the stairs, craning his neck, wistfully, to see them to the last minute.* SAM *and* MARY *enter.*)

SAM

Well, sir, h'observin' somethin' of partikler interest?

PICKWICK

(*Sadly*)

Sam, there are moments when I almost wish I were more than an observer.

(PICKWICK *turns and walks disconsolately into the kitchen.*)

MARY

Your master, Mr. Weller?

SAM

My employer. I'm thought to be my *own* master, my dear. (*He goes over to the table and discovers the brandy*) Ah, here's luck! Drink with me, my chick.

MARY

(*Coy*)

I an't got a glass.

SAM

No glass needed, my dear. Put your lips to this 'ere tumbler and then I can kiss you by deputy.

MARY

Oh, for shame, Mr. Weller!

SAM

What's a shame, my dear?

MARY

Talkin' in that loose way . . .

SAM

Nonsense—kissin' an't no harm. It's nature, an't it?

MARY

Is it, Mr. Weller?

SAM

Well, if it an't, it oughter be. . . . After I get Mr. Pickwick into his jacket, I'll be out for the evenin'. Are you h'occupied, my dear?

MARY

Occupied, Mr. Weller?

SAM

Thet's it.

MARY

I suppose I could ask my master, Mr. Wardle.

SAM

Now if *I* was your master I'd take great comfort in't.

MARY

Lor', Mr. Weller—would you now?

SAM

I would, thet.

(MR. STIGGINS *enters very unsteadily, wanders over to a table and slumps down.* SAM *turns back to* MARY.)

SAM

Walk out with me for half an hour?

MARY

Ssh! They's someone present.

(*Points to* MR. STIGGINS.)

SAM

Him? He an't present. Will you walk out?

MARY

(*Going to door*)

Well, I might walk out for a bit of air, bein' it's you, Mr. Weller—and most likely I won't be seein' you again.

SAM

(*Following her*)

Thet's yet to talk on!

(*As they get to the door,* PICKWICK *enters from the kitchen.*)

PICKWICK

Sam!

SAM

(*From doorway*)

H'occupied, sir! Back in a jiffy, sir!

(SAM *hurries out with* MARY.)

PICKWICK

(*Calling after him*)

Sam!

(PICKWICK *shrugs, turns, and starts for the stairs, when* MR. STIGGINS *rouses himself and speaks, staring straight ahead.*)

STIGGINS

Vanity! All ish vanity!

PICKWICK

(*Startled, turning back*)

Sir? (STIGGINS *makes no reply*) Were you addressing me, sir? (*Still no reply.* PICKWICK, *annoyed, comes down to him*) You *spoke* to me, sir, did you not?

STIGGINS

All ish vanity.

(*He leans forward uncertainly.*)

PICKWICK

(*Sternly*)

You are inebriated, sir!

STIGGINS

On the contrary, temperanch man, my friend. Sh-pend whole life—fighting—scourge of liquor. S'truth!

PICKWICK

But, sir, I can smell your breath!

STIGGINS

Orange—sch'peel, sir. Orange sch'peel soaked in rum. S'periment, sir. Science.

PICKWICK

(*Interested*)

A scientific experiment?

STIGGINS

'Zackly. Better to know whash I'm up against, sir.

PICKWICK

(*Whipping out his notebook*)

Very interesting. Do tell me, sir, what have you gleaned from your study of orange peel soaked in rum? In short, scientific intoxication—how does it make you feel?

(*A pause.*)

STIGGINS
(*Finally*)
Happy.

PICKWICK
Happy.
(*Starts to write.*)

STIGGINS
Happy—in an odious way.

PICKWICK
Odious, sir?

STIGGINS
Odious—in a happy way.

PICKWICK
(*Frowning*)
That—that—seems a bit confusing to me, sir.

STIGGINS
Very-y confusing.

PICKWICK
(*Putting notebook away*)
I think I shall not record that, sir.

STIGGINS
Do ash you like.

(PICKWICK *takes up the glass of rum and orange peel and sniffs it. He is about to lift it to his lips when the other Pickwickians stroll in, notebooks still in hand.*)

TUPMAN
Are you making an observation, Pickwick?

PICKWICK

I am, sir. Orange peel, soaked in rum. What do you think of that?

(TUPMAN *takes it up, smells it, passes it to the others.*)

TUPMAN

I *love* orange peel!

STIGGINS

(*Gravely*)

So do I.

(*At this moment* SAM, *followed by a dry, bustling little man,* MR. PERKER, *enters.* PERKER *carries a large letter in his hand.*)

PERKER

Ah, Mr. Pickwick! Here you are. Been searching for you everywhere! Very disturbing news!

PICKWICK

Dear me, what?

PERKER

Dreadful. Shocking. As your lawyer, had to seek you out. You're being sued!

PICKWICK

Sued! Good heavens, Mr. Perker! By whom?

PERKER

(*Holding up letter, reading almost with pleasure*)

Sir,

Having been instructed by Mrs. Martha Bardell to commence an action against you for a breach of promise of marriage, for which the plaintiff lays her damages at fifteen hundred pounds—we beg to inform you that a writ has been issued against you in this suit in the Court of Common Pleas, and request to know by return of post the name of your attorney in London who will accept service thereof.

We are, Sir,
Your obedient servants,
Dodson and Fogg

(PICKWICK *stands bewildered*)

Monstrous, isn't it? Extraordinary case. Your opponent has chosen the best legal firm in London. Great prestige. (PICKWICK *still does not speak*) A base conspiracy, sir! A vile attempt to extort money! What shall we do?

TUPMAN

Better get up to London, Pickwick.

WINKLE

Yes, face it out!

SNODGRASS

Take some action!

PICKWICK

(*Horrified*)

Action? But, gentlemen, I am innocent!

PERKER

What's your point, sir? This is a legal action. (*He calls*) Sam!

SAM

Sir?

PERKER

Get places on the London coach.

SAM

Very good, sir.

PICKWICK

No! (*Suddenly*) No, Sam. Wait! (SAM *turns back*) I—I—can't go tomorrow.

PERKER

*Can't* sir? Why not, sir?

PICKWICK

(*Very tentative*)

I—I should have to break a promise. I should—have to abandon Mrs. Leo Hunter's breakfast party.

PERKER

(*Snorting*)

Breakfast party, sir? Breakfast party! Don't you understand, sir—you're being sued!

SAM

An't you never been sued before, Sir?

PICKWICK

N— no.

PERKER

Well, then, sir?

PICKWICK

(*Wistful, uncertain*)

But I—I've never been to a breakfast party, either!

*CURTAIN*

# ACT 1

## SCENE III

*SCENE: The breakfast party on* MRS. LEO HUNTER'S *lawn. In the foreground, right, is a haystack with a garden seat in front. Left, one side of a bright-colored tent which extends on to the stage. A refreshment stand, right. Rear, a small platform for recitations, and right of the platform a sandbox and shooting stand. A target can be seen in the distance. This entire area is surrounded by a wooden fence, with an entrance gate, right. Rolling green hills stretch away in the distance. The whole effect is festive and full of the spirit of a late summer lawn party.*

*All the guests are in costume except the Pickwickians and* MR. STIGGINS. MRS. LEO HUNTER *is Minerva;* MISS RACHEL WARDLE *is a lady of fashion. The* WARDLES *are all present, also* MR. JINGLE, MR. PERKER, *and others.*

*AT RISE:* SNODGRASS *is completing the recitation of his quatrain from the platform. The guests stand in front of him.*

SNODGRASS

"Stroud, Rochester, Brompton and Chatham,
We have been in 'em and we have been at 'em,
And all we've seen is here verbatim,
Of Stroud, Rochester, Brompton and Chatham!"

(*Applause.* SNODGRASS *steps down and* MRS. HUNTER *promptly springs to the platform.*)

MRS. HUNTER

Our *sincerest* thanks to the esteemed members of the Pickwick Club for *sharing* with us—at the Delphic Den—Mr. Snodgrass, today's poet!

(*Gentle applause.*)

PICKWICK

(*Stepping forward*)

And now, ma'am, will you oblige us by reciting your "Ode to an Expiring Frog"?

MRS. HUNTER

(*Whipping a paper out of her bosom*)

Sir, if you insist. (*Clears her throat with elaborate preparation*) There are two succinct verses. To be sure, my little effort renders itself somewhat better when accompanied by the strains of the harp. But—as we are *without* harp this morning, I shall *try*—alone—alone! (*She holds up the paper to read*) Ode—to an—Expiring—Frog! (*At this moment, the band, which is somewhere in the tent, strikes up a tune.* MRS. HUNTER *looks up, annoyed*) Mr. Pickwick, pray ask them to cease playing! (PICKWICK *hurries over to the tent and gestures tentatively to the band*) The band! So *energetic*! Every *one* an artist, you know!

(PICKWICK *returns, looking forlorn. The band is still playing.*)

PICKWICK

How, Madam, does one stop a band?

MRS. HUNTER

(*Shouting imperiously toward the tent*)

Band! Band! *Stop!* (*The band stops abruptly.* MRS. HUNTER *arranges her face once more for recitation*) Now the first verse! Ode—to an—*Expiring—Frog!*

"Can I view thee panting, lying
On thy stomach, without sighing,
Can I unmoved see thee dying
On a log
Expiring frog!"

(MRS. HUNTER *pauses. Gentle applause.*)

PICKWICK

What a tender sentiment!

RACHEL

Most touching!

(MRS. HUNTER *holds up her hand for silence.*)

MRS. HUNTER

The last verse is said to be *still* more touching. Shall I repeat the first—or just *plunge* on?

TUPMAN

If you please, ma'am, plunge on.

(MRS. HUNTER *frowns, then quickly raises her paper again.*)

MRS. HUNTER

"Say, have fiends in shape of boys,
With wild halloo, and brutal noise,
Hunted thee from marshy joys
With a dog,
Expiring frog!"

(*The applause starts hesitantly, then gains in vigor;* MRS. HUNTER *bows and stuffs the poem back into her bosom where there appears to be unlimited space. Some of the audience move forward and shake her hand.*)

PICKWICK

Very finely expressed, ma'am.

TUPMAN

Most pleasantly melancholy, ma'am.

SNODGRASS

And, as you say, very succinct. *Very* succinct. May I have a copy?

MRS. HUNTER

(*Promptly reaching into her costume and pulling out a huge bundle*)

With pleasure. Delighted.

(*She starts to distribute the poem.*)

SNODGRASS

Thank you. I am honored.

(*When the distribution is over,* MRS. HUNTER *holds up her hand and calls vigorously.*)

MRS. HUNTER

Now to the games! Games! *Every*body! Into the tent, if you please. The first game—my *own* creation—"Pinning the Word on Plato." For this occasion my dear husband has kindly consented to act as Plato. (*She calls*) Wilburforce! Wilburforce! (WILBURFORCE *hurries forward*) Into the tent! *Come! Come,* everybody!

(*The Guests move into the tent—all except* PICKWICK, RACHEL, JINGLE; *and* SAM, *who stands in the background.*)

PICKWICK

(*Calling after* RACHEL)

Miss Wardle!

RACHEL

(*Turning back*)

Sir?

PICKWICK

Do you really want to Pin the Word on Plato?

JINGLE

(*Quickly*)

Shouldn't desert party, Pickwick, old boy. Very impolite.

(*He takes* RACHEL'S *arm.*)

RACHEL

(*To* PICKWICK)

Mr. Jingle has fittingly reminded me, sir . . .

JINGLE

(*Hurrying her into the tent*)

Sorry, old fellow. The proprieties, you know.

(RACHEL *and* JINGLE *go into the tent.* PICKWICK *looks after them, very unhappy.*)

SAM

(*Coming over slowly*)

Vell, you looks sad, guv'nor. Anythin' wrong?

PICKWICK

Sam, I would share a secret with you.

SAM

If you share it, 'tain't a secret no longer. But go ahead.

PICKWICK

(*Looking round cautiously*)

Sam, I'm so confused I think I *may* be—in love!

SAM

*May* be? Don't you know straight out?

PICKWICK

No, I don't.

SAM

Then it's a quandary, as the feller said.

PICKWICK

Precisely.

SAM

Hmm . . . May I call to your attention, sir, you're bein' sued and breached by one lady already?

PICKWICK

Ah, I know. Poor Mrs. Bardell. Poor misguided soul. But I've no doubt that unfortunate matter will right itself . . . Sam, tell me, have you ever made your heart known to any—fair lady?

SAM

You mean, has I proposed or any sich radical maneuver?

PICKWICK

Yes. Have you ever—*ever* . . .

SAM

Never! Though I've made a considerable few of 'em think it might be in the offing.

PICKWICK

(*Disappointed*)

Then you've no idea how it's best to begin in these matters?

SAM

Best not to begin a'tall, sir.

(*At this moment* SNODGRASS, *blindfolded and carrying a large sign in his hand, with the word THINK on it, staggers out of the tent and gropes forward. Several of the guests follow him out, laughing most merrily.*)

SNODGRASS

Hot or cold?

MRS. HUNTER

(*With shrill joviality*)

*Cold,* Mr. Snodgrass! *Freezing!* You'll never, never find Plato out *here*!

(*She turns him round. They all disappear again, with much giggling, into the tent.*)

PICKWICK

Sam, I'm in trouble.

SAM

So's Mr. Snodgrass, if you ask me.

PICKWICK

Naturally! Mr. Snodgrass is a poet, and poets—Sam, surely you've formed *some* idea on how to approach matrimony?

SAM

A few, sir. But rarely has I submitted 'em to the gruesome test of experience.

PICKWICK

Just the same, I'd be very obliged to you for . . .

SAM

(*Thoughtfully*)

Well, to sum up at the beginning, I'd say—don't be too hasty. Or as a Pickvickian might put it, "Look before you leaps."

PICKWICK

(*Writing this down*)

Ah, yes, to be sure.

SAM

In other words, don't start right out maulin' or grabbin' or fussin' about the female too much.

PICKWICK

(*Startled*)

Bless me, Sam, such a thought never occurred to me!

SAM

Well, does to some.

PICKWICK

Mauling and grabbing! Can such things be?

SAM

They can. In fact—but never mind. Fer *you,* go at it gradual.

PICKWICK

Indeed, yes. I shall.

SAM

Commence, sir—with mebbe a high tribute to the lady's h'imperious bewty and excellent qualities—if she has any.

PICKWICK

Oh, she has, Sam. She has! (*Band starts up and* PICKWICK *and* SAM *have to shout*) SHE COLLECTS MOTHS, SAM!

SAM

WOT?

PICKWICK

MOTHS. SHE COLLECTS THEM.

SAM

WOT FOR?

PICKWICK

(*Shouting in imitation of* MRS. HUNTER)

Band! Band! *Stop!* (*The band stops abruptly.* PICKWICK *looks pleased*) I've changed, Sam. I'm far more—more *commanding,* wouldn't you say?

SAM

Possibly, sir.

PICKWICK

As I was saying, Sam, this lady—she collects moths for science. The pursuit of science.

SAM

Well, I hope for your sake she catches up to it! Is it Miss Wardle yer a'thinkin' on, sir?

PICKWICK

It is.

SAM

(*Frowning*)

H'mm.

PICKWICK

What would you do next, Sam?

SAM

. . . Vell, if you're obliged to persevere in this 'ere business . . . and I see you are—I'd hint next at my own unworthiness. How I was a brute and not worth touchin' the hem of her garment and all such whiffle as thet.

PICKWICK

Whiffle, Sam?

SAM

Whiffle, sir. Howsomever I wouldn't say too *much* about unworthiness. That's jist to get her softened up. Unworthy for *her* only, so to speak—but a very desirable object fer anybody else.

PICKWICK

(*Eagerly recording this*)

Yes! Yes!

SAM

By way of provin' that, I'd make a brief runover of my past life and present condition—puttin' both of my best feet forwards, so to speak.

PICKWICK

Very good.

SAM

This is a purty slow method—but thorough. (*Pauses*) Then you might get back to speakin' again of the warmth of yer love and the depth of yer devotion . . .

PICKWICK

True. And then?

SAM

And then per'aps you might be tempted to seize her hand . . .

PICKWICK

(*Very excited*)

Indeed, yes! That would be a very good point!

SAM

If thet's goin' smooth, then come to the plain and simple question.

PICKWICK

What's that, Sam?

SAM

Will yer or won't yer?

PICKWICK

What a moment! What a thrilling moment!

SAM

I think I can safely predict—as public figures all says—as how a woman who collects moths might, at this 'ere moment, modestly turn away her head.

PICKWICK

You think that action may be taken for granted?

SAM

I do, sir.

PICKWICK

Because if she did not do that at the right place, it would be most embarrassing.

SAM

(*Confidently*)

She'll do it. And ven she does, I'd squeeze her hand.

PICKWICK

Again?

SAM

You didn't squeeze it the first time—you only took it.

PICKWICK

(*Referring to his notes*)

Oh, yes. So I did.

SAM

If after that darin' move you meet with no stoppages, you should draw away, gentle-like, the handkerchief which my knowledge of human nature tells me the lady would be applyin' to her eyes about this time, and steal a respectful kiss.

PICKWICK

Kiss her? Bless my heart, Sam—that's progress!

SAM

Progress! Thet's the whole thing!

PICKWICK

But there must be more!

SAM

No more *I* can tell yer. It's every man for hisself from then on!

PICKWICK

Am I to understand that after kissing her she would doubtless murmur into my ears a bashful acceptance?

SAM

Thet might be it. Thet's one re-h'action.

PICKWICK

(*Enthusiastically*)

Sam, you're a genius! I'll seek the lady out this minute!

SAM

Will you be a-needin' of me, sir? If not, I might take the h'opportunity to find out some results of my own along the same general line.

PICKWICK

Results, Sam?

SAM

Between me and thet 'andsome young female I been poppin' out with.

PICKWICK

Oh to be sure. Do you find you have—things in common?

SAM

(*Dryly*)

More or less.

PICKWICK

Is her mind interesting, Sam?

SAM

It may be, sir—though she ain't had a chance to use it overmuch as yet.

PICKWICK

Have you seized her hand yet?

SAM

I have.

PICKWICK

Have you stolen a respectful kiss?

SAM

I have.

PICKWICK

(*Eagerly*)

With what results?

SAM

She bit me.

PICKWICK

Bless me! What if Miss . . .

SAM

She won't.

PICKWICK

Dear me! I trust not.

(*At this moment* JINGLE *and* RACHEL WARDLE *appear.*)

JINGLE

Glorious party, Miss Wardle—capital songs—capital company —excellent time—very! (*Sees* PICKWICK) Ah, friend Pickwick!

(MRS. LEO HUNTER *bursts in followed by* WINKLE *who carries his fieldpiece. The other guests also trail in.*)

MRS. HUNTER

(*Catching sight of* RACHEL *and* PICKWICK)

Come, Miss Wardle! Come, Mr. Pickwick! Gentlemen! No missing *any* of the events!

WINKLE

Yes, Pickwick—mustn't miss this one!

PICKWICK

(*Frowning*)

Winkle, *what,* pray, is your intention?

WINKLE

To shoot, sir.

MRS. HUNTER

Mr. Winkle has gallantly offered to give us a demonstration of his marksmanship. The poetry of mechanism!

(WINKLE *arranges himself at the shooting stand. Everyone gathers round.*)

PICKWICK

Winkle, are you sure you wish to go on with this—this action?

WINKLE

I am as weary of observation as you, sir.

MRS. HUNTER

Go stand near the target, Mr. Pickwick, and call out the results!

PICKWICK

(*Severely*)

Winkle, I do this only to spare you embarrassment. I have *seen* you shoot, sir. Pray excuse me, Miss Wardle.

(*He starts off for the target, rear.*)

WINKLE

(*Raising his gun awkwardly*)

Has anyone a particular preference—the red, the blue, or the white?

MRS. HUNTER

Oh, do try for the eye of the bull, Mr. Winkle!

WINKLE

Try, ma'am! Why, I could do it blindfolded, ma'am.

PICKWICK

*(Calling impatiently)*

Then do it! Do it! And get it over with!

MRS. HUNTER

*(Shouting)*

Do call the score so we can all hear, Mr. Pickwick.

(WINKLE *aims, pulls the trigger, there is only a click.*)

WARDLE

What's the matter? Won't it go?

WINKLE

Bad weapon. Missed fire.

WARDLE

*(Taking gun)*

Odd.

*(Examines gun)*

Why, look, man, you've left off the cap!

WINKLE

Bless my soul! I declare, I forgot the cap!

*(He produces a cap, places it in the gun and aims again. This time when he fires there is a scream in the distance. They all gasp and look toward the target.)*

WARDLE

*(Running forward)*

Good heavens! *Pickwick!*

*(The other guests follow.)*

RACHEL

(*Fearfully, to* JINGLE)

What has happened, sir?

JINGLE

Wrong target—rum go—poor old boy! (RACHEL *shrieks then promptly faints.* JINGLE *carries her to the garden bench where he bends over her*) Come now—nothing to it—*clean* death—once in India . . .

(*At this point the guests reappear above the shooting stand with* PICKWICK *in the lead. His face is stormy, as he advances holding out his hat, which has a hole in it.*)

PICKWICK

(*To* WINKLE)

Wretch! My hat!

WINKLE

I'm sorry, Pickwick. Fearfully sorry.

PICKWICK

*Sorry,* sir? Look at this hat! It might have been my head!

WINKLE

But it wasn't.

PICKWICK

Do you realize, sir, that your unprofessional marksmanship has debased our club standing?

WINKLE

(*Bristling*)

Sir, my marksmanship is beyond question!

PICKWICK

It is indeed! Very *far* beyond.

WINKLE

If I failed the target, sir, it was obviously a fault of the mechanism. At any rate, sir, it was an accident.

PICKWICK

I'm most pleased to hear, sir, that it was not intentional.

RACHEL

(*Reviving*)

Is he *wounded*? Is he *dead*?

PICKWICK

Dear, dear madam, calm yourself. I am unhurt.

RACHEL

Oh, say you are not dead!

WARDLE

Don't be a fool, Rachel. What the devil's the use of his *saying* he isn't dead?

MRS. HUNTER

Come! (*Gesturing to them all*) Come! All! Put this little incident behind you! Mr. Winkle has shot! Mr. Pickwick has recovered! Come! On with the morning schedule! Next, the boating events! *Boat-ing! Boat-ing!*

(*She motions them all into the distance.*)

PICKWICK

Ma'am, at this moment I fear I am not equal to the boating.

RACHEL

Nor I, ma'am.

MRS. HUNTER

Then, Mr. Pickwick, you and Miss Wardle are generously excused from the aquatics.

PICKWICK

(*Bowing*)

Thank you, ma'am.

MRS. HUNTER

Come! *Boat*-ing. *Boat*-ing.

(MRS. HUNTER *departs, with the crowd following her off.* WINKLE *stops a moment before leaving.*)

WINKLE

(*Solicitously*)

Are you quite certain you're all right, Pickwick?

PICKWICK

(*Sternly*)

I am, sir. But may I remind you, sir, in the future—"Look—before you shoot"!

(WINKLE, *very downcast, starts off again, then turns back peevishly.*)

WINKLE

I *did* look.

(WINKLE *goes off.* PICKWICK *and* RACHEL *are left alone on the garden bench, though* JOE, *the Fat Boy, sits up once in this interval and shows himself to be still resting on the haystack.*)

RACHEL

(*Taking up* PICKWICK'S *battered hat*)

What a pity, sir. I hope you are not too shaken?

PICKWICK

Oh, it's nothing, nothing, ma'am. I should much prefer at this moment to hear more about your moths.

RACHEL

(*Lyrically*)

Oh, lovely moths! Lovely moths! Where shall I begin, sir?

PICKWICK

Oh, begin—any lepidopterous insect will do, ma'am.

RACHEL

You are so understanding. I think I shall start with the hawkmoth. Have I mentioned the hawkmoth?

PICKWICK

The hawkmoth? I think not, ma'am.

RACHEL

It always sounds so savage! Don't you love it? With its toothed spines it can lacerate the rind of fruits. Lacerate!

PICKWICK

Indeed! (*Glances cautiously at his notebook, then mumbles aloud*) "Not too hasty. Then both feet forward."

RACHEL

Have I your interest, sir?

PICKWICK

(*Looking up quickly*)

Entirely, ma'am. I was just glancing over my notes on the subject . . . Miss Wardle, you are an angel!

RACHEL

(*Startled*)

Mr. Pickwick! *Sir!*

PICKWICK

Nay, I know it but too well!

(*At this moment* JOE *sticks his head over the top of the hayrick directly behind* PICKWICK *and* RACHEL *and observes them broodingly.*)

RACHEL

All women are angels, they say.

PICKWICK

Do they? Dear me! (*Looks at notes again*) Then what can *you* be? Or to what, without presumption, can I compare you? (RACHEL *remains blushfully silent*) Where was the woman ever seen who resembled you? Where else could I hope to find so rare a combination of excellence and beauty? Where else could I seek to . . . (*Refers to notes, then changes his voice*) Oh, I am not worthy to touch the toe of your shoe!

RACHEL

Men are such deceivers.

(JINGLE *appears in the background and watches scene unobserved.*)

PICKWICK

But not all men, ma'am. There lives at least one being who can never change—one being who would be content to devote his whole existence to your happiness—who lives but in your eyes—who breathes but in your smiles—who bears the heavy burden of life itself only for you!

RACHEL

Could such an individual be found?

PICKWICK

He *can* be found! He *is* found! Miss Wardle, he is *here.*

(PICKWICK *falls on his knees, where he takes another quick look at his notes, as* RACHEL *turns away.*)

RACHEL

Mr. Pickwick, rise.

PICKWICK

Never. (*He seizes her hand, then throws his notes away entirely*) Oh Rachel! Say you return my ardor!

(*Kisses her hand.*)

RACHEL

(*Her face still averted*)

Mr. Pickwick—I cannot listen! I cannot speak!

PICKWICK

Dear girl! Do speak! Speak!

RACHEL

Sir, possibly I can safely say that I am not—not *wholly*—indifferent to you! (PICKWICK, *encouraged, leans forward and gives her a peck on the cheek.* RACHEL, *after a moment, returns the peck. They embrace. At this moment* JOE, *the fat boy, sneezes. Startled,* PICKWICK *and* RACHEL *jump back.* RACHEL *turns in alarm and sees* JOE) Mr. Pickwick—we are observed! We are *discovered*!

PICKWICK

(*Sternly*)

What do you want here, boy?

JOE

(*Fearfully*)

Nothin', sir. Nothin' at all.

PICKWICK

Then have the goodness to leave.

JOE

Y-yes, sir. Right away, sir.

PICKWICK

And Joe . . .

JOE

Yes, sir?

PICKWICK

I shall have a present for you tomorrow, my boy.

JOE

Yes, *sir*. Thank 'ee, sir.

(JOE *runs out.*)

RACHEL

(*Frantically*)

Oh dear! Oh dear, dear, dear!

PICKWICK

Don't fret yourself, my love. The boy knows nothing. And if he does, I—I, for one, am not ashamed before the whole world!

(JINGLE'S *face appears again at the arbor window.*)

RACHEL

But my nieces—they're heartless! They'll laugh at me! And my brother may be mortally wounded!

PICKWICK

Why, pray? My intentions are honorable.

RACHEL

Oh, I know, I know—but these embraces and—and kisses . . . they throw such a different light on everything!

PICKWICK

Do they? Oh dear—I thought that the best part of it!

RACHEL

My brother will think it a scandal—to have reached such intimacy in such a brief time.

PICKWICK

Don't fret, my angel. I'll search out the boy. I'll see that he reveals nothing until you are ready to speak your heart boldly. (*He starts off*) I shall return immediately, my love. Immediately!

(*He blows her a kiss and goes out.* JINGLE, *the instant* PICKWICK *has left, steps from the shadow of the arbor and hurries over to* RACHEL.)

JINGLE
(*With affected earnestness*)
Miss Wardle, forgive intrusion—no time for ceremony—all discovered!

RACHEL
Sir!

JINGLE
(*Whispering*)
Hush! Large boy—dumpling face—round eyes—rascal.

RACHEL
(*Trying to appear composed*)
I presume you allude to Joseph, sir?

JINGLE
I do, ma'am—treacherous dog, Joe—on his way to tell your brother—kissing and hugging—ah, ma'am—eh?

RACHEL
Mr. Jingle, if you came here, sir, to insult me . . .

JINGLE
By no means, ma'am. Passed boy—overheard tale—tender my services—prevent the hubbub . . .

RACHEL
(*Bursting into tears*)
Oh dear! My brother will be angry!

JINGLE
Furious!

RACHEL

Oh, Mr. Jingle, what *can* I do? Help me!

JINGLE

Pooh, pooh! Say the boy dreamt it; nothing more easy—blackguard boy—lovely lady—fat boy horsewhipped—end of the matter!

RACHEL

Oh, sir, you *are* reassuring!

JINGLE

Nothing to it, ma'am. Leave all to me! (*He sighs heavily and turns away*) Ahhhh! To me! Mercy—mercy . . .

(*Sighs again.*)

RACHEL

(*Startled*)

What, sir? You seem suddenly stricken.

JINGLE

Stricken, ma'am! Desolate—done—extinct!

RACHEL

Sir, may I show my gratitude for your kind interference in my dilemma by inquiring into the cause of your unhappiness, with a view to its removal?

JINGLE

(*After a quick look to see if he is observed*)

Ha! Removal! Remove *my* unhappiness. Impossible! Have you not just bestowed your love upon a man who is insensible to the blessing—who even now contemplates a design upon the affections of the niece of the creature who, to me . . . ! But no, he is my friend. I will not expose his weakness, his vices. Miss Wardle—farewell!

(JINGLE *applies a handkerchief to his eyes and starts off.*)

RACHEL

Stay, Mr. Jingle!

JINGLE

(*Stopping short*)

Stay?

RACHEL

Sir, you have made an allusion to Mr. Pickwick. Pray explain the remark.

JINGLE

Never! Never! I must go!

(*He drops immediately onto the garden bench and leans nearer* RACHEL.)

RACHEL

(*Anxiously*)

Mr. Jingle—I entreat—I implore you—if there is any mystery connected with Mr. Pickwick, reveal it.

JINGLE

O heartless avarice! Can I see—lovely creature—sacrificed at shrine—(JINGLE *appears to be struggling with conflicting emotions, but suddenly he straightens and speaks bluntly*) Ma'am, Pickwick only wants your money! (RACHEL *is shocked*) You do *have* money, don't you? (RACHEL *nods.* JINGLE *looks pleased*) Not only money. More than that—Pickwick loves another.

RACHEL

Another! Who?

JINGLE

Short girl—black eyes—your niece Emily.

RACHEL

Emily! No! It can't be!

JINGLE

You possess a Bible, ma'am?

RACHEL

Certainly, sir.

(*She produces a small Bible.*)

JINGLE

(*Quickly, laying his hand on it*)

God's truth! So help me!

RACHEL

(*Overcome*)

Oh, oh, it is too much! Too much!

JINGLE

Sad. Very sad. But life— Don't be duped, ma'am. Watch 'em.

RACHEL

(*Stiffening, suddenly determined*)

I will.

JINGLE

Watch his looks.

RACHEL

I will.

JINGLE

He'll flatter her.

RACHEL

Flatter her! Let him!

JINGLE

He'll pay her every possible attention.

RACHEL

Let him.

JINGLE

And he'll cut you.

RACHEL

Cut *me*! Cut *me,* will he?

JINGLE

You must show your spirit.

RACHEL

I will.

JINGLE

And not have him afterwards?

RACHEL

Never!

JINGLE

Stout girl. Bravo! You'll consider another, then? (*Immediately,* JINGLE *drops on his knees, still keeping his eye out for other guests*) I am on my knees, ma'am.

RACHEL

So I see, sir.

JINGLE

Affection has brought me here.

RACHEL

Rise, Mr. Jingle.

JINGLE

Why, ma'am?

RACHEL

We are out of doors, sir.

JINGLE

Cruel charmer! You—who since the moment of our meeting—cast me adrift—alone—on the open sea of love . . .

RACHEL

How you run on, sir!

JINGLE

Run on? Nothing to the hours, days, weeks, months, years, when we're united. Run on—they'll fly on—volt—mizzle—steam engine—thousand horsepower—nothing to it!

(*He kisses her hands.*)

RACHEL

Mr. Jingle, dear sir, you are so tempestuous.

JINGLE

I am! I am!

RACHEL

If Mr. Pickwick proves false—if his perjury be made clear and manifest . . .

JINGLE

Then you are mine! Marry tomorrow!

(*Seizes her hands again and kisses them with a great show of passion.*)

RACHEL

(*Gasping*)

Oh! Oh! I feel faint! Sir, I am not accustomed to—to such unbridled passion. Pray, guide me to my brother, Mr. Jingle.

(*They start off arm in arm just as* PICKWICK *enters.*)

PICKWICK

Thought you were at the boating, Mr. Jingle?

JINGLE

(*Breaking away*)

Beautiful day. Spring in my blood—restless as a hound dog.

PICKWICK

Where are you off to, Miss Wardle?

(RACHEL *sweeps haughtily past* PICKWICK *and out.* PICKWICK *stands bewildered.*)

JINGLE

(*Turning back*)

Don't worry, old boy. Lady upset. Everything known. (*Guides* PICKWICK *over to a corner, then speaks softly*) Don't trust fat boy. Scoundrel.

PICKWICK

But I just paid him a guinea!

JINGLE

Too late. Take other course. Avert suspicion. Miss Wardle's earnest wish.

PICKWICK

What do you mean?

JINGLE

A strategy, sir. Merely a temporary course. Deceive the brother—all your attention to the *niece*—rather rude, than otherwise, to the *aunt*—only way. Dissemble! Play the part! Throw 'em off scent! (PICKWICK *seems hesitant*) Miss Wardle insists . . . Dissembling, too. But sends her love. Unalterable affection and so forth.

PICKWICK

(*Fervently, grasping* JINGLE'*s hand*)

My dear fellow, carry my best affection to her.

JINGLE

Done.

PICKWICK

Say it will be hard to dissemble.

JINGLE

Anything more?

PICKWICK

Say how ardently I long for the time when I may call her mine, and all deceit may be unnecessary.

JINGLE

Stout fellow. Well said.

PICKWICK

Oh, my friend! Receive my dearest thanks for your disinterested kindness.

JINGLE

On the contrary, *most* interested, old boy. Most interested.

PICKWICK

My dear friend, how can I ever repay you?

JINGLE

Don't speak of it. (*He stops short*) On second thought—how's for ten pounds? (PICKWICK *frowns*) Very particular purpose. Pay you in three days. Three. No more. All over then. No more difficulties.

PICKWICK

(*Reaching for purse*)

Ten pounds. I daresay I can spare that.

(PICKWICK *counts out the money. The guests begin to appear in the background.* SNODGRASS *with* EMILY, TUPMAN *and* ISABELLA, MRS. LEO HUNTER.)

JINGLE

Bless you, old boy. (*Pocketing money*) Be careful. Remember! Not a look to Miss Wardle.

PICKWICK

Not a look.

JINGLE

Not a word.

PICKWICK

Not a syllable.

JINGLE

Not a whisper.

PICKWICK

Not a sound.

JINGLE

Excellent!

(JINGLE *starts to go just as* MRS. LEO HUNTER *sweeps in with the other guests.* RACHEL *is on her brother's arm.*)

MRS. LEO HUNTER

Stay, Mr. Jingle. (*She faces them all*) Attention—everybody! The next event will be the *sing—ing*! Inside the tent—everyone! Choose your partners for the choral *sing—ing*!

PICKWICK

(*Starting forward instinctively, his arm extended toward* RACHEL)

Miss Rachel—? (*He stops, suddenly remembering, and turns away*) I mean—Miss Emily, my dear?

(*He offers his arm to* MISS EMILY, *who looks startled, but takes it. They march off.*)

RACHEL

(*Staring after him in horror, gasping*)

Oh! Oh! Deceiver!

(*She leans back heavily on her brother, almost fainting.* JINGLE *rushes over.*)

JINGLE

You see, Miss Wardle? Old boy, young girl. Just as I said! (*He offers* RACHEL *his arm*) This arm—always yours, ma'am!

RACHEL

You are most gallant, sir.

MRS. LEO HUNTER

That's right, Mr. Jingle. Take your partner. Take your partners. (*The guests start off.* WILBURFORCE *lags behind and drops wearily on the garden bench.* MRS. HUNTER *seizes his arm*) Come, my dear. Don't be faint-hearted! Only five more events until breakfast!

(*She marches imperiously toward the tent, pulling her husband after her as the band strikes up.*)

*THE CURTAIN FALLS*

# ACT 2

# ACT 2

## SCENE I

*SCENE: The Inn of Act One, the following evening.*

SAM WELLER, *with ink and quill, is laboriously scratching away at some mysterious piece of writing. A moment later his father enters.*

MR. WELLER

Vell, Sammy.

SAM

(*Laying down his pen*)

Vell, my ancestor. What's the last bulletin about stepmother?

MR. WELLER

Mrs. Veller passed a wery good day, but is uncommon unpleasant this evenin'—signed upon oath, Tony Veller, Esquire, Senior.

SAM

An' thet red-nosed feller?

MR. WELLER

Still here, Sammy. And when he's not, he's sich a friend o' the family he can't bear to leave us without takin' somethin' from the cellar to remember us by. (*Notices* SAM's *writing*)

Wot's that you're a-doin' of? Pursuit of knowledge under difficulties, Sammy?

SAM

(*With some embarrassment*)

Seein' as 'ow Mr. Pickwick moves up to London tomorrow for his lawsuit, I've been a-writin' wot I ain't had time to say.

MR. WELLER

Not writin' to any young woman, I hopes, Sammy?

SAM

Vy, it's no use a-sayin' it an't. It's a walentine, guv'nor.

MR. WELLER

A walentine! It an't Walentine's Day and won't be for nine months!

SAM

All the more reason why it will make a startlin' impression.

MR. WELLER

(*Reproachfully*)

Nevertheless, Samivel, I didn't think you'd ha' done it.

SAM

Vy not?

MR. WELLER

Arter all the warnin' you've had! Arter all I've said upon this 'ere wery subject! After actiwally seein' and bein' in the company o' your stepmother vich I should ha' thought was a moral lesson as no man could never ha' forgotten to his dyin' day! I didn't think you'd ha' done it, Sammy. (*Lights his pipe*) It's wery agonizin' to me at my time of life—seein' my own flesh and blood approachin' the treacherous rocks.

SAM

I an't a-goin' to get married, guv'nor. I'm just preparin' the ground fer future dewelopments. I'll read you the walentine— an' you can judge of it fer yourself.

MR. WELLER
(*Settling back*)

Fire away.

SAM

(*Holding up the valentine self-consciously, finally reading*) "Lovely . . ."

MR. WELLER

Stop! (MR. WELLER *rings the bell on the table*) I can't go no further 'thout a stimulant . . . Now thet first word, Samivel —"lovely"—wery strong. Wery strong sentiment.

SAM

I'm jist puttin' down my real feelin's.

MR. WELLER

Thet's what's so worrisome about it.

(MRS. WELLER *enters*.)

MRS. WELLER
(*Sharply*)

Well, you?

MR. WELLER

A double glass o' the inwariable, my dear.

MRS. WELLER

Wot's the matter? Lost yer locomotion?

(*She goes out*.)

MR. WELLER

Y'see, Sammy? Y'see how married people grows together?

SAM

She's bringin' it, an't she?

MR. WELLER

She is thet—but vill I know whether it's rum or pisin?

SAM

You'll know ven you drink it.

(MRS. WELLER *returns and puts a drink before him.*)

MRS. WELLER

There! And I hope it gives you a stroke!

MR. WELLER

Thank 'ee, my dear. It's not the gift, it's the spirit of the thing.

MRS. WELLER

Don't be talking to me, you brute! You'll provoke me to forget my sex and strike you.

MR. WELLER

I an't sayin' a word, my dear. Not a word. Go on, Sammy.

(MRS. WELLER *goes out.*)

SAM

(*Reading*)

"Lovely creetur . . ."

MR. WELLER

Tain't poetry, is it?

SAM

No, no.

MR. WELLER

Wery glad to hear it. Poetry's unnat'ral. Never you let yourself down to talk poetry, my boy. Begin again, Sammy.

SAM

"Lovely creetur, I feel myself a-damned . . ."

MR. WELLER

(*Interrupting*)

Hold! That an't proper.

SAM

No, it an't "damned"—(*Holds paper up to the light*) It's "ashamed," there's a blot there—"feel myself ashamed and completely para—" I forget wot this 'ere word is.

MR. WELLER

Vy don't you look at it then?

SAM

So I am a-lookin' at it, but there's another blot.

MR. WELLER

Pity it an't all blots.

SAM

"Paraphrased"—thet's it. "I feel myself ashamed and completely paraphrased in addressing of you, for you *are* a nice creetur and nothin' but it."

MR. WELLER

Still dangerous—but a wery pretty sentiment.

SAM

(*Pleased*)

Yes, I think it *is* rayther good.

MR. WELLER

Wot I likes in thet 'ere style of writin' is thet there an't no callin' names in it—no Wenuses, nor nothin' o' thet kind. Wot's the good o' callin' a young woman a Wenus or a angel, Sammy?

SAM

Ah, wot indeed, if she an't?

MR. WELLER

Drive on, Sammy.

SAM

(*Reading*)

"Afore I seen you, I thot all women wuz alike."

MR. WELLER

So they are. Drive on.

SAM

(*Reading*)

"But now I find wot a reg'lar soft-headed, inkred'lous turnip I must ha' been, for there an't nobody like you, though I like you better than nothin' at all." (*Looks up*) I thought it best to make that rayther strong.

MR. WELLER

You succeeded uncommon well, my boy.

SAM

(*Reading*)

"So I take the privilege, my dear—as the gen'l'm'n in difficulties did when he killed hisself one Sunday—to tell you thet the first and only time I seen you, your likeness took on my heart in much quicker time and brighter colors than ever a likeness was took by the profeel macheen—which perhaps you have heerd on, Mary my dear—although it *does* finish a portrait and put the frame and glass on complete, with a hook at the end to hang it by, and all in two minutes and a quarter . . ."

MR. WELLER

That last part—I'm afeerd that werges on to so much unnat'ral meanin' as to be close to the poetical Sammy.

SAM

No it don't. Listen to the rest of it. (*Reads on quickly*) "Accept of me, Mary my dear, as your walentine and think over wot I've said. My dear Mary, I will now conclude." (*Looks up*) Thet's all.

MR. WELLER

(*Startled*)

That's raythen a sudden pull-up, an't it, Sammy?

SAM

Not a bit on it. She'll wish there wuz more—and that's the great art o' letter writin'.

MR. WELLER

Well, I wish yer stepmother 'ud only conduct her conwersation on the same gen-teel principle. You a-goin' to sign this walentine?

SAM

I am thet. I'm signin' it Veller.

MR. WELLER

Won't do.

SAM

Vy not?

MR. WELLER

Never sign a walentine with yer own name, Samivel. Sign any good name, but never yer own. S'pose you signs it Pickwick—thet's a wery good name and a easy one to spell.

SAM

So 'tiz.

MR. WELLER

You've nothin' to lose thet way. Or nothin' to gain, as the case may be.

SAM

(*Writing*)

How's this—"To Mary—your lovesick Pickwick."

MR. WELLER

Wery good. You want me to deliver this 'ere document for you personal, Samivel?

SAM

No, I don't.

MR. WELLER

Don't you trust me, son?

SAM

Vell, guv'nor . . .

MR. WELLER

(*Happily*)

You're a good judge of human nature, my boy. I'm proud of you.

SAM

Vell, you've been a good father, old 'un—never given me no help o' any kind, thereby allowin' my natchural genius to flower. (*At this moment* MARY *enters briskly from the outside and crosses to the stairs without looking at them.*) Good evenin', my pretty.

MARY

Good evenin', gentlemen. (*She gets to the stairs*) Good night, gentlemen.

(SAM *runs and catches her arm.*)

SAM

Hold up there!

MARY

(*To* SAM)

Why, Mr. Weller! Whatever is agitatin' you?

MR. WELLER

It's the summer heat, my dear. Pay no attention to anythin' the boy says.

SAM

I've somethin' to give you, my chick.

(*Holds out the valentine.*)

MARY

A letter, Mr. Weller? Now whoever would be a-writin' to me?

SAM

You never knows till you gets to the bottom, as the feller said ven he fell into the well.

(MARY *opens the valentine and scans it.*)

MARY

(*Blushing*)

Lor'! Why it's—it's from Mr. Pickwick!

(*She seems happily confused.*)

SAM

(*Eagerly*)

Wot does it say?

MARY

Oh, it says—oh it's bewtiful!

SAM

(*To* MR. WELLER)

You see, guv'nor?

MARY

Lor'. Lor', who'd a thought Mr. Pickwick . . .

MR. WELLER

He's known to be a gentleman of romantic nature, my dear. It wouldn't be anythin' like love that he'd be a-writin' of, would it?

SAM

(*Sternly*)

Guv'nor, don't you feel the arms of Morphine a-callin' you?

MR. WELLER

Can't say as I do. Howsomever, it's uncommon plain I *ought* to. (*Starts off*) Good night, my boy. And think on yer step-mother. Keep her face afore you.

(MR. WELLER *goes out.*)

SAM

Vell, my pretty?

MARY

Well what, Mr. Weller?

SAM

I hope my walentine h'expresses some sentiments I an't otherwise said.

MARY

*Your* valentine, Mr. Weller? Do tell. This, sir—is from Mr. Pickwick, as you very well know.

SAM

Pickwick Weller, my dear. It's of my own composin' and all done 'thout eny outside help.

MARY

I don't believe it!

SAM

Who else but me could a-put so many purty thots on you into so little ink?

MARY

(*Airily*)

Who else? Oh, quite a few, Mr. Weller. Quite a few.

SAM

(*Bristling*)

Is thet so?

MARY

You don't think you're the only gentleman what has taken notice of me, do you now?

SAM

If that's your h'attitude afore the tenderest thots of a man's heart, you can return the missile to the sender.

(*He snatches the valentine out of her hand. At this moment* WARDLE *and* PICKWICK *enter, talking together, from the outside.*)

PICKWICK

Good evening, Sam. Mary.

SAM

'Evenin', sirs.

MARY

(*Blushing, curtseying*)

'Evenin', sirs. (*She comes over to* PICKWICK *timidly*) Mr. Pickwick?

PICKWICK

Yes, my dear?

MARY

(*Curtseying again*)

Beggin' your pardon, sir, I wish to ask you . . .

(SAM *suddenly grabs her and yanks her out of the door.*)

PICKWICK

Bless me! What do you make of that, Wardle?

WARDLE

Sir, I've long ceased trying to comprehend the actions of creatures under the age of twenty-five! (*Eyes* PICKWICK *sharply*) By the bye, sir, I notice *you* had your eye on my daughter Emily yesterday. You sly old dog!

PICKWICK

Wardle, I have a confession to make.

WARDLE

Good. Always enjoy a good confession. Few enough of 'em down here in the country.

PICKWICK

You must tell no one.

WARDLE

Trust me, Pickwick.

PICKWICK

I hope you will understand what I'm going to say.

WARDLE

I hope so.

PICKWICK

I hope you will not be offended.

WARDLE

I hope not.

PICKWICK

This can bring us closer together.

WARDLE

I hope so.

PICKWICK

Or make us further apart.

WARDLE

I hope—good Lord, Pickwick, *tell* me!

PICKWICK

A member of your family has touched my heart—romantically.

WARDLE

(*Sternly*)

Now, Pickwick, you know I am very fond of you. We are about the same age. Have the same friends in London and so forth.

PICKWICK

True.

WARDLE

You notice I say *we* are the same age?

PICKWICK

I do, sir.

WARDLE

Well, sir?

PICKWICK

Go on, sir.

WARDLE

These things seldom work out, Pickwick. An old boy and a young thing. Comes to grief. Besides, are you certain the girl returns your affection?

PICKWICK

I am, sir.

WARDLE

(*Startled*)

Bless me! She does?

PICKWICK

She does, sir.

WARDLE

Pickwick, it won't do.

PICKWICK

(*Weakly*)

You don't approve? Wardle, my dear friend, you've got to allow the girl her life.

WARDLE

It's not so much that, sir, but Emily is . . .

PICKWICK

Emily, sir! I speak of *Rachel,* your sister.

WARDLE

Rachel!

PICKWICK

Yes, dear girl. We are betrothed.

WARDLE

(*Seizing* PICKWICK'S *hand with great warmth*)

Pickwick! My friend! My dear old friend! Welcome to the family!

PICKWICK

You approve then? You don't mind giving her up?

WARDLE

Giving her up? Approve? Pickwick, I support! I encourage! I—sympathize. I—I am at your service, sir! How soon's the wedding?

PICKWICK

Personally, I have no wish to delay one instant.

WARDLE

Good! Good! (*Turns to him*) But tell me, my dear fellow, if you're so gone on Rachel, why were you making eyes at Emily this morning?

PICKWICK

A strategy, sir. A strategy to guard our secret.

WARDLE

Well, I declare! It was well played, old boy.

PICKWICK

I hope you will forgive my deceit.

WARDLE

(*Warmly*)

Forgive! My dear Pickwick, I am in your debt! Do come and have a glass with me—before we retire.

(*They walk toward stairs.*)

PICKWICK

I trust you will not miss your sister too much. I feel as if I've been waiting for her all these years.

WARDLE

Well, she's done a bit of waiting herself.

PICKWICK

Has she? Dear girl. Wardle, this has relieved my conscience.

WARDLE

My dear fellow, it has relieved me, too.

(*They move up the stairs and out as the scene darkens.*)

(*The room is empty for a moment, then* SAM *and* MARY *enter, rear, from their walk.*)

SAM

Vill you sit a minute, my dear?

MARY

There an't no light in here, Mister Weller.

SAM

And there an't *goin'* to be none!

MARY

Lor', why not?

SAM

I prefers things as they are fer my conwersation. Here. Over here, my chick.

(*They seat themselves behind the bench just as* JOE, *the* FAT BOY, *wanders on.*)

JOE

Is thet you, Mr. Weller?

SAM

(*Stern*)

Joe, vy an't you in bed?

JOE

I an't sleepy—for *onct*! Why are you over there a-sittin' in the dark? Don't you want a candle?

SAM

No! We don't! (JOE *continues to stand without moving*) Joe, there's a fresh pie in the kitchen.

JOE

(*Brightening*)

There is?

SAM

Vell, don't ye vant it, little one?

JOE

I *wants* it, but I'm afraid to go out there 'thout a candle.

SAM

Yer a wery big help to me, Joe. (*To* MARY) My dear, we're a-goin' to the kitchen to get Joe h'occupied.

MARY

Whatever *for,* Mister Weller?

SAM

You'll see! (*He pulls* MARY *up, then motions to* JOE) Come on, you. And listen hard now—ven yer finishes this 'ere morsel, I wants yer to start another!

JOE

*Two* pies! Thet's very nice of you, Mister Weller. Thank 'ee.

SAM

Yer velcome. But keep eatin'.

(*They go out. Immediately* MR. JINGLE's *head appears at the door, rear. He enters cautiously, carrying two traveling cases.* MR. STIGGINS *stumbles on with him.*)

JINGLE

(*Whispering*)

Careful, Mr. Stiggins! No noise—else devil of a rumpus! (JINGLE *turns to stairs and calls softly*) Hurry, my love. Minutes are hours until you are mine.

STIGGINS

Is the lady a church member?

JINGLE

Oh, certainly—certainly—long standing—both are.

STIGGINS

Very good.

(RACHEL *enters dressed for traveling.*)

RACHEL

Oh, Mr. Jingle—I am so agitated. Should I drop my veil?

JINGLE

(*Eyeing her critically*)

Yes, drop it. By all means. (*He starts across the door*) You are acquainted with the Reverend Mr. Stiggins, my dear?

RACHEL

Indeed, yes. (JINGLE, *at the door, peers out cautiously, assembles the bags, disappears into the entrance way.* RACHEL, *during this interval, turns to* MR. STIGGINS. MARY *and* SAM *re-enter from the kitchen—then stop short*) How is your health, sir?

STIGGINS

Improved, ma'am.

RACHEL

Have you tried a brandy tonic, sir, when you feel unsteady?

STIGGINS

Never!

RACHEL

Then you must let me prepare it for you when the occasion offers. Excellent remedy, sir. (*At this remark,* STIGGINS *crosses and kisses her on the cheek.* RACHEL *looks pleased, but startled*) Dear me, sir! And you a member of the *cloth*!

STIGGINS

The "kiss of peace"! Do not be alarmed, ma'am. Merely a spiritual acknowledgment of your sympathy.

(*Bends toward her again.*)

JINGLE

(*Entering*)

Come now. None of that, Mr. Parson. *After* ceremony! Must be off, my dear. Everything ready—coach to fly in—shepherd to marry us—license to seal it—love to live by . . .

(*They all go out. The stage is empty for a moment. Then, outside, voices can be heard, and the creaking of a coach.* SAM, *followed by* MARY, *sprints wildly up the stairs.*)

SAM

(*Calling*)

Mr. Pickwick! Mr. Wardle! Sirs! Sirs! (*A stir above and voices, off stage*) Downstairs! Hurry! (SAM *races back across the stage and out, still calling*) Mr. Pickwick! Mr. Wardle!

(*The stage is again empty, but running footsteps can be heard on the stairs.* PICKWICK *and* WARDLE, *half dressed, enter, carrying candles, just as* SAM, *with difficulty, hauls* JINGLE *into the Inn.* RACHEL *follows them.* SNODGRASS *enters from stairs.*)

WARDLE

(*Startled*)

Well, what's all this?

PICKWICK

Yes, what?

(*A pause.*)

WARDLE

Come, speak up, Rachel.

(WINKLE *and* TUPMAN *enter from stairs.*)

JINGLE

(*Coolly*)

Miss Wardle and I are off to be married.

WARDLE

Married!

SAM

Case o' love at second sight!

PICKWICK

But Rachel . . .

RACHEL

(*To* PICKWICK)

Cruel deceiver!

PICKWICK

(*Advancing on* JINGLE)

You villain! You've hypnotized her! (SNODGRASS *steps over and catches* PICKWICK's *arm*) Let me at him, sir!

SNODGRASS

Calm yourself, Pickwick.

PICKWICK

(*Raging*)

Let me at him, I say!

JINGLE

My dear sir, pray consider. Strike a man—what follows? Law suit—defamation of character—action for damages . . .

PICKWICK

Damages! I should warrant, sir, there'll be damages! Let me at him!

(SAM *is now also engaged in holding off* PICKWICK.)

WARDLE

I'll handle this, Pickwick. Do hold up, old boy.

PICKWICK

Scoundrel! He should be indicted!

WINKLE

Imprisoned!

TUPMAN

Hanged!

WARDLE

(*To* JINGLE)

Well, sir—how dare you drag my innocent sister from her bed?

JINGLE

Drag, sir? Innocent, sir? The lady is enamored.

WARDLE

Nonsense. (*Turning to* RACHEL) Rachel, what do you mean—running away with this vagabond. Take off that veil and go to your room this instant!

JINGLE

Do nothing of the kind, my love.

WARDLE

What arrogance!

PICKWICK

Outrageous!

JINGLE

Lady's free to act as she pleases—more than one-and-twenty.

WARDLE

(*Explosively*)

More than one-and-twenty! More than one-and-forty!

RACHEL

(*Indignantly*)

I am not!

WARDLE

You *are*! You're fifty if you're an hour!

(RACHEL *shrieks and sinks into a chair as though fainting.* PICKWICK *hurries to her.* MRS. WELLER *rushes in.*)

MRS. WELLER

What's all these goings-on in a respectable house?

TUPMAN

A glass of water! Water, landlady!

WARDLE

Aye, bring a bucket and throw it all over her!

MRS. WELLER

(*To* WARDLE)

You brute! Are you the lady's husband? (*She takes a carafe of water from the table, pours a glass and gives it to* RACHEL, *who is now sunk so deep in her chair as to be hidden from view*) Poor dear. Come now, drink a bit of this. There's a love.

PICKWICK

(*Anxiously*)

Hadn't we better transport her upstairs, Wardle? Look how pale she is!

JINGLE

(*Stepping over*)

Who dares take her away—unless she wishes it?

RACHEL

(*Momentarily reviving*)

I *won't* be taken away! I *don't* wish it!

(RACHEL *subsides again.* JINGLE *stands looking defiantly at* WARDLE *and* PICKWICK.)

PICKWICK

(*To* JINGLE)

You owe me ten pounds, sir! I'm now prepared to take it from your hide!

WARDLE

Pickwick, I beg you, let me settle this. (*To* JINGLE) A word with you, sir.

JINGLE

Willingly. Where there's a word there's a way.

(*The three draw to one side.*)

WARDLE

Pray sit down, sir.

JINGLE

Prefer to stand—active—restless character.

PICKWICK

Wretch!

TUPMAN

Scoundrel!

WINKLE

Villain!

WARDLE

Do control yourselves, gentlemen. (*To* JINGLE) Now, sir, we know that you are running off with my sister for the sake of her money. Very good. But the fact is, sir, beyond a hundred pounds or so, the lady has little or nothing until the death of her mother. A fine old lady, her mother.

JINGLE

*Old,* you say?

WARDLE

Rather old, sir, as families go. But mark me, since Julius Caesar invaded England, only one of our family has not reached eighty-five—and he was beheaded.

JINGLE

The old lady's present age?

WARDLE

Seventy-three. (WARDLE *takes a pinch of snuff and offers some to* PICKWICK, *who refuses*) So I put it to you, wouldn't fifty pounds and liberty be better than my sister and expectation?

(*A pause.*)

JINGLE

(*Finally, coolly*)

Won't do. Not enough.

PICKWICK

Wretch! Cad!

WARDLE

Well, we won't waste time splitting hairs, eh? Just tell me what is enough. (WARDLE *sits at a table and draws out a cheque, flourishes a quill pen, and waits*) Just tell me, sir.

JINGLE

(*Frowning*)

Expensive affair. License, three pounds. Hiring of coach, five pounds. Breach of honor—loss of lady . . .

PICKWICK

Never mind the last two items, sir!

WARDLE

Say a hundred pounds?

JINGLE

And twenty.

WARDLE

(*Beginning to write cheque*)

Very well. A hundred and twenty. I'll make it payable, sir, the day after tomorrow, by which time, sir, you will be out of the county, I trust.

(*Hands cheque to* JINGLE *who pockets it calmly.*)

PICKWICK

And now, sir, have the goodness to leave this place instantly!

JINGLE

(*Coolly*)

Off directly. (*Tosses a paper on the table*) Here, old sport—marriage license— get name altered— do for you.

(JINGLE *goes out.* PICKWICK *leaps forward after him.* SAM *catches* PICKWICK *in mid-air.*)

SAM

Here now! Hold *up,* sir!

PICKWICK

Let me at him!

SAM

What's the use of runnin' with legs like yours after a man with legs like thet? Save your vinegar, sir—with a breach of promise ahead of you, you've need of it!

WARDLE

(*Turning, startled*)

A breach of promise! Why, what's this, Pickwick?

PICKWICK

(*Humbly*)

Wardle, I have been falsely accused.

WARDLE

Of what?

PICKWICK

Of promising to marry a certain lady in London.

(RACHEL *sits up straight.*)

WARDLE

Indeed!

PICKWICK

I go to court on the morrow to defend myself.

RACHEL

(*Shrieking again*)

Oh! Oh, perfidious man! Ohhhhh!

(*She collapses again.*)

PICKWICK

(*Rushing over to her*)

Wardle! Look! She's fainted again!

(WARDLE *walks over and peers down at her.*)

WARDLE

(*Calm*)

She'll come around.

PICKWICK

(*Anxious*)

Will she? Are you certain?

WARDLE

Well, she always *has*!

(PICKWICK *gazes down at her unhappily as*

*THE CURTAIN FALLS*

# ACT 2

## SCENE II

*A courtroom in London. The* JUSTICE's *stand is left and a little to the rear. The* USHER *or Clerk's stand is also left, below the* JUSTICE. *The witness box, a kind of pulpit with a brass rail, is center. Two tables, one down left, one down right, with two empty chairs each, are for the use of the defendant and his barrister. The tables are provided with foolscap, ink bottles and quill, water pitcher and mug, and many large, red-sealed documents. Extreme right are rows of seats for the spectators—about two rows visible with an aisle down the center. Entrances to the courtroom are down the aisle and back of the Judge's stand. The jury is to the right, indicated by a row of twelve hats.*

*The courtroom is empty except for the* USHER, *who is asleep at his stand.* PICKWICK *and* PERKER *enter at once.* PICKWICK *surveys the scene with mingled curiosity and apprehension.*

PICKWICK
(*Pointing*)
That's the witness box, I suppose?

PERKER
That's the witness box.

PICKWICK
And that—that's where the jurymen sit, is it not?

PERKER

The identical place. Your first lawsuit, eh, Mr. Pickwick?

PICKWICK

(*Warmly*)

You know very well it is, sir!

PERKER

I mention the fact only by way of instructing you, sir, to be calm.

PICKWICK

And when, sir, have I been otherwise? (PERKER *frowns and begins to tap his snuffbox*) You seem nervous, Mr. Perker.

PERKER

I was wondering what the foreman of the jury has had for breakfast.

PICKWICK

And is that pertinent, sir?

PERKER

Indeed, yes. Highly important. A hungry juryman always finds for the plaintiff.

PICKWICK

Bless my heart! Why should that be?

PERKER

If he's hungry he wants to get it done with and get home to his dinner.

PICKWICK

(*Indignantly*)

But justice . . .

PERKER

Don't speak of it here, sir. We are in court. (*Rises*) Ah, here they are at last!

(MRS. BARDELL, *dressed in black and supported by* MRS. CLUPPINS, *comes down the aisle and is led to her chair by* BUZFUZ. TOMMY *is clinging to his mother's skirt.* BUZFUZ, *having arranged* MRS. BARDELL *in a drooping state, hands her an oversized umbrella and a pair of pattens.* MRS. BARDELL, *after being seated, suddenly rouses from her stupor and kisses* TOMMY *frantically.* BUZFUZ, *rubbing his eyes very hard with a large white handkerchief, gently pulls the clinging boy away and guides him down to* MRS. CLUPPINS *in the spectators' seats. All this is highly calculated to appeal to the pity of the jury and spectators. The other spectators*—WINKLE, SNODGRASS, TUPMAN, *the* WARDLES, MR. STIGGINS, SAM, *etc.—begin to enter.*)

BUZFUZ

(*Cordially, to* PERKER)

Good morning, sir.

PERKER

(*Equally amiable*)

Good morning.

BUZFUZ

Very fine morning, sir.

PERKER

Very fine indeed.

PICKWICK

(*Astonished*)

And who, sir, is that gentleman who just said it was a fine morning?

PERKER

Mr. Serjeant Buzfuz. Our opponent. He leads for the other side.

PICKWICK

(*Outraged*)

Our opponent! Then why, sir, did you . . .

(*At this moment the* USHER *holds up his hand and bellows loudly.*)

USHER

Silence! Silence!

(PICKWICK *jumps, startled.* JUSTICE STARLEIGH, *barely visible under his great wig, enters from the rear and seats himself fussily. The spectators and all others in the courtroom rise at his entrance.*)

Oyez! Oyez! His Majesty's Court is now open!

(*All sit. The* JUSTICE *brings down his gavel. The courtroom is silent.*)

JUSTICE

Bardell versus Pickwick. Who is for the plaintiff?

BUZFUZ

(*Rising*)

I am, My Lord. Mr. Buzfuz.

JUSTICE

(*Writing*)

For the plaintiff, Mr. Fuzbuz.

BUZFUZ

Buzfuz, Your Worship.

JUSTICE

(*Irritably*)

Buzfuz, Fuzbuz—what difference? (*He glares down*) For the defendant?

PERKER

(*Rising*)

Mr. Perker, My Lord.

JUSTICE

(*Writing name down*)

Mr. Jerker for the defendant.

PERKER

Begging Your Lordship's pardon, Perker—Perker!

JUSTICE

Oh, very good. Never had the pleasure of hearing the gentleman's name before. (*Turns to* BUZFUZ) Open for the plaintiff, sir.

(BUZFUZ *turns to* MRS. BARDELL, *whispers something, pats her shoulder consolingly, straightens his gown, settles his wig, and turns toward the court.*)

BUZFUZ

My Lord—and distinguished gentlemen of the jury—never in the whole course of my professional experience—never, from the very first moment of applying myself to the study and practice of the law—have I approached a case with feelings of such deep emotion. This is an action, gentlemen, for a breach of promise of marriage, in which the damages are laid at fifteen hundred pounds. What are the facts and circumstances of the case?

PICKWICK

(*Leaping up*)

What, indeed?

(PERKER *pulls him down quickly.*)

JUSTICE

(*Rapping gavel*)

Silence!

BUZFUZ

(*Glaring at Pickwick*)

I shall overlook this grave discourtesy on the part of the defendant. It springs, no doubt, from apprehension. (*Turns back to court*) The facts, gentlemen, you shall now hear detailed by me, and proved by the unimpeachable and saddened female whom I will place in this box before you. (*At the word "box," he smacks the table vigorously*) The plaintiff, gentlemen—the plaintiff is a widow.

JUSTICE

(*Writing*)

A widow?

BUZFUZ

Yes, Your Lordship, a widow. The late Mr. Bardell, after enjoying for many years the esteem and confidence of his sovereign as one of the guardians of the royal revenues, glided almost imperceptibly from this world, to seek elsewhere for the repose and grace which a custom-house can never afford . . .

MRS. BARDELL

Beggin' yer pardon, sir—Mr. Bardell died o' bein' knocked on the head with a quart pot.

BUZFUZ

(*His voice faltering momentarily*)

Yes, we know, ma'am. *How* he died is of no great matter. (*He recovers his poise and turns back to the Court*) The point, sirs—the point is—before this good man's death, he had stamped his likeness on a little boy. (*Gesturing to* TOMMY, *who stares back like a gargoyle*) With this dear little boy, Mrs. Bardell, the plaintiff, shrank in her sorrow from the world and courted the retirement and tranquillity of Gosbridge Street . . .

MRS. BARDELL

Gos-*well* Street it wuz . . .

BUZFUZ

(*Barely controlling his temper*)

Yes, yes, we know, ma'am. The street is of no great matter.

JUSTICE

She *shrank* from Gos*well* Street, then?

BUZFUZ

Yes, Your Lordship. I shall now call my client. (*Comes over to* MRS. BARDELL) Come, my dear. Are you strong enough to go to the witness box?

MRS. BARDELL

(*Springing up*)

I kin manage.

(*The* USHER *catches her in passing, draws her aside to be sworn in. The "swearing in" is very fast and unintelligible, but we see* MRS. BARDELL *kiss the Bible fervently before proceeding to the witness box.*)

JUSTICE

Give the Court your name, ma'am.

MRS. BARDELL

H'an't you got it already? (*Points to* BUZFUZ) He's said it nigh on to five times.

JUSTICE

(*Sternly*)

Your name, ma'am. And be quick about it.

MRS. BARDELL

Martha Bardell—but they calls me Mattie.

BUZFUZ

Now, Mrs. Bardell—in Gos-*well* Street, in July of this year, did you not place a placard in your front parlor window?

MRS. BARDELL

Yes, Your Worship, sir.

BUZFUZ

What *inscription* did this placard bear?

MRS. BARDELL

(*Puzzled*)

Don't know as it bore anythin' like *thet,* sir.

BUZFUZ

(*Patiently*)

What "writing" was on the placard?

MRS. BARDELL

(*Rattling it off*)

"Apartment furnished for a single gentleman. Inquire Within."

BUZFUZ

(*Triumphantly*)

Ah, note that, My Lord and jury! "Apartment furnished for a *single* gentleman!" Mr. Bardell had once been a "single gentleman" himself, had he not, ma'am?

MRS. BARDELL

(*Nodding*)

He had thet!

BUZFUZ

Mr. Bardell was a man of honor, a man of his word, no deceiver. To whom, then, but to a "single gentleman" did this innocent woman turn in her desolation? What a beautiful and touching impulse! But with what terrible consequences!

MRS. CLUPPINS

Terrible! Terrible!

JUSTICE

Silence!

BUZFUZ

(*Turns back to* MRS. BARDELL)

Now, Mrs. Bardell, tell us how long did the sign remain in the window?

MRS. BARDELL

Three days, I think 'twuz. Anyways, it warn't fly-specked when it was took down.

BUZFUZ

Only three days, gentlemen! Why? Because the serpent was on the watch.

MRS. BARDELL

(*Bristling*)

Don't be callin' me no serpent, sir!

BUZFUZ

The reference was not to you, ma'am. (*Turns back to jury*) After three days, gentlemen, a being, erect upon two legs, and bearing all the outward semblance of a man and not of a monster, knocked at the door of this good woman's house, and took the lodgings. This man was— (*He refers to his papers to find the name*) Pickwick—Samuel Pickwick, the defendant! (BUZFUZ *pauses for breath and surveys his effect*) Of this man, Pickwick, I will say little.

JUSTICE

(*Yawning*)

Good.

BUZFUZ

The subject presents but few attractions—and I, gentlemen, am not the man, nor are you, gentlemen, the men, to delight in the contemplation of revolting heartlessness and systematic villainy.

PICKWICK

(*Leaping to his feet*)

What's that, sir?

(PERKER *pulls him down again, with difficulty.*)

USHER

Order! Order!

JUSTICE

Proceed, Mr. Buzfuz.

BUZFUZ

And now, gentlemen, here are two letters that passed between the defendant and the plaintiff. (*He produces the letters*) They are not open, fervent, eloquent, epistles, breathing the sincere language of affectionate attachment. No, they are sly and underhanded, calculated to mislead any third party. Yet they speak—*volumes*!

(*He smacks the table again.*)

MRS. CLUPPINS

(*From a spectator's seat*)

Read 'em!

JUSTICE

(*Sternly*)

No comment is warranted from the spectators.

BUZFUZ

My Lord, I offer these letters into evidence as marked exhibits. (*Hands letter to* MRS. BARDELL) Mrs. Bardell, read this letter, pray.

MRS. BARDELL

(*Squinting*)

It says: "Dear Mrs. B.: Chops and tomater sauce. Yours, Pickwick."

BUZFUZ

There, gentlemen! "Chops and tomato sauce. Yours, Pickwick." What does this mean?

JUSTICE

Well—what *does* it mean?

BUZFUZ

Terms of endearment, My Lord. Chops—gracious me! Tomato sauce! Gentlemen, is the happiness of a trusting widow to be trifled away with such idle language of love?

JUSTICE

(*Curtly*)

Pray read the second letter.

BUZFUZ

No *date* on this one—which is in itself suspicious. (*He reads*) "Dear Mrs. B. I shall not be at home till tomorrow. Slow coach."

(*Glances around triumphantly.*)

MRS. CLUPPINS

That an't all of it!

(BUZFUZ *throws her a stern look.*)

BUZFUZ

And then, gentlemen, there follows this most remarkable expression. "Don't trouble yourself about the warming-pan." Ha! The warming-pan! Think of that!

JUSTICE

(*Writing*)

Warming-pan.

BUZFUZ

Why, gentlemen, who *does* trouble himself about a warming-pan? When was the peace of mind of men, or women, broken or disturbed by a warming-pan, which is in itself a harmless, a useful, and I will add, gentlemen, a comforting article of domestic furniture? What, then, is behind this word? Is it a mere cover for hidden fire? (*He laughs shortly at his own joke*) Or is it actually contrived by Pickwick with a view to hinting of his desertion?

MRS. BARDELL

Mr. Pickwick allays asked for a warmin' . . .

BUZFUZ

(*Interrupting*)

Pickwick, gentlemen, Pickwick, the ruthless destroyer of this domestic oasis in the desert of Goswell Street—Pickwick, who has choked up the well and thrown ashes on the sward—Pickwick, who comes before you today with his heartless tomato sauce and warming pans—Pickwick still rears his head with unblushing effrontery and gazes without a tremor on the ruin he has made. The *ruin,* gentlemen!

(*All turn and look at* MRS. BARDELL, *who indeed at this moment, with her hat awry and her hair frumped out, does somewhat resemble a ruin*)

You may step down, Mrs. Bardell.

MRS. BARDELL

(*Disappointed*)

Is that all? You told me a-plenty more to say!

BUZFUZ

That will be all, Mrs. Bardell. (*Helps her down, then turns to jury*) I shall now summon Mrs. Elizabeth Cluppins.

(PERKER *now is bending over* PICKWICK *who is bristling with indignation.* MRS. CLUPPINS *bustles forward, very agitated, and goes through the same mumbo-jumbo swearing in with* USHER *and kisses Bible*)

MRS. CLUPPINS

(*Pointing to witness box*)

Up there?

BUZFUZ

If you please, ma'am. (MRS. CLUPPINS *takes the stand and promptly bursts into tears*) Pray compose yourself, ma'am. You are here in the interest of justice.

MRS. CLUPPINS

(*Wiping her eyes*)

My feelin's is too many for me.

JUSTICE

Your name, madam?

MRS. CLUPPINS

Elizabeth McTavish Cluppins, M'Lord.

BUZFUZ

Now, Mrs. Cluppins, do you recollect being in Mrs. Bardell's sitting-room on one particular morning of July last, when she was called to Pickwick's apartment?

MRS. CLUPPINS

I remember and recollects it, both.

JUSTICE

What were you doing in the sitting-room, ma'am?

MRS. CLUPPINS

My Lord and jury, I had been out with me basket to buy three pound of red kidney purtaties, which was tuppence ha'penny, when I sees Mrs. Bardell's street door on the jar.

JUSTICE

On the what?

BUZFUZ

Partly open, my lord.

JUSTICE

She *said* on the jar.

MRS. CLUPPINS

I walked in, gentlemen, just to say good mornin'. There was the sound of voices in the front room, and . . .

BUZFUZ

And you listened, I believe, Mrs. Cluppins?

MRS. CLUPPINS

*(Majestically)*

Beggin' your pardon, sir—I would scorn the h'action! The voices was uncommon loud and forced themselves upon my ear.

BUZFUZ

*(Patiently)*

Well, Mrs. Cluppins, you were *not* listening but you heard the voices, nevertheless?

MRS. CLUPPINS

That's it. I heard 'em!

BUZFUZ

Was one of those voices Pickwick's?

MRS. CLUPPINS

It were, sir.

BUZFUZ

What was this Pickwick saying?

MRS. CLUPPINS

Never mind whut he was sayin', when I come into the room he was embracing my friend Mrs. Bardell in his *arms*!

(PICKWICK *springs to his feet to protest.*)

RACHEL

*(From audience, shrieking)*

Ohhhh . . .

JUSTICE

Silence!

BUZFUZ

That will be all, Mrs. Cluppins.

MRS. CLUPPINS

(*Taking no notice*)

I've this to add—as the mother of eight children and with confident expectation of presentin' Mr. Cluppins with a ninth . . .

JUSTICE

You may omit your interesting family history, ma'am. (*To* PERKER) Any questions from the other side?

PERKER

(*Rising as if to say something, then thinking better of it*)
No questions, M'lud!

PICKWICK

(*Indignantly*)

Why not, sir?

PERKER

(*Softly*)

Strategy, Pickwick. Strategy.

(PICKWICK *scowls and remains silent.*)

BUZFUZ

(*To* MRS. CLUPPINS)

That will be all, Mrs. Cluppins. (MRS. CLUPPINS *reluctantly returns to her seat*) Next witness, Samuel Weller.

MRS. CLUPPINS

(*To the* JUDGE—*as she crosses*)

I could tell you a-plenty more!

(SAM *is on his feet and into the witness box almost as soon as his name is announced. He places his battered hat on the floor and his arms on the rail, then faces the court with great assurance and cheerfulness.*)

USHER

The witness is not sworn, sir.

SAM

Never swear. It's agin my principles.

JUSTICE

(*Severely*)

You must take oath, my man.

PICKWICK

(*To* PERKER)

Perker, can't you offer something in my defense?

PERKER

In due time, sir.

(SAM *is sworn in, after which he goes into the witness box.*)

BUZFUZ

You are Mr. Samuel Weller?

SAM

One o' the truest things spoke by you for many a long year! Samuel Veller—that's the monicker!

JUSTICE

(*Writing*)

Do you spell your name with a V or a W?

SAM

Depends on the taste and fancy of the speller, My Lord. I never had occasion to spell it more'n once or twice, but I spells it with a Wee.

(*A voice in the rear, that of* SAM's *irrepressible father, calls out.*)

MR. WELLER

Quite right, Samivel, quite right! Put it down a Wee, My Lord, put it down a Wee!

JUSTICE

(*Peering out, startled*)

Who is that who dares address His Majesty's Court? Usher, bring that person here instantly! (*There is a great commotion, and everyone peers down the spectators' aisle, but the* USHER *finds no one. The* JUSTICE *turns back to* SAM) Do you know who that was, sir?

SAM

(*Coolly*)

I rayther suspect it was my father, My Lord.

JUSTICE

Do you see him here now?

SAM

(*Gazing at the ceiling*)

No, I don't, My Lord.

JUSTICE

Proceed, Serjeant Buzfuz.

BUZFUZ

Now, Mr. Weller.

SAM

Now, sir!

BUZFUZ

I believe you are in the service of Mr. Pickwick, the defendant in this case. Speak up, if you please, Mr. Weller.

SAM

I means to speak up, sir. I *am* in the service o' that 'ere gentleman, and a wery good service it is.

BUZFUZ

(*With forced jocularity*)

Little to do and plenty to get, I suppose?

SAM

Oh, quite enough to get, sir, as the burglar said ven he blew open the lawyer's safe.

JUSTICE

You must not tell us what the—er—burglar, or any other man said. What the burglar said isn't evidence.

SAM

Wery good, My Lord. That's evident.

BUZFUZ

Do you recollect anything happening on the morning when you were first engaged by the defendant, eh, Mr. Weller?

SAM

Yes, sir, I do.

BUZFUZ

Have the goodness to tell the jury what it was.

SAM

I had a reg'lar new fit-out o' clothes that mornin', gentlemen of the jury.

BUZFUZ

(*Patiently*)

I mean, Mr. Weller, any *uncommon* circumstance. . . .

SAM

A new fit-out o' clothes wuz a very uncommon circumstance with me in those days, sir!

(*Laughter in court. The* JUSTICE *raps his gavel.*)

JUSTICE

(*Severely, to* SAM)

You had better be careful, sir.

SAM

So Mr. Pickwick said at the time, My Lord. And I was very careful o' that 'ere suit o' clothes. Wery careful indeed, My Lord.

(*The* JUSTICE *for a full minute looks sternly at* SAM *whose gestures remain calm and serene. The* JUSTICE *finally motions to* BUZFUZ *to proceed.*)

BUZFUZ

Do you mean to tell me, Mr. Weller, that you saw nothing of this scene, the plaintiff in the arms of the defendant, which you have heard described by a witness?

SAM

I did not. I wuz outside until they called me in, and when I come in, the old lady wuz not there.

MRS. CLUPPINS

Who's an old lady?

USHER

(*Rapping gavel*)

Silence in the court!

BUZFUZ

Now attend, Mr. Weller—you were there, and yet you saw nothing of what was going forward? Have you a pair of eyes, Mr. Weller?

SAM

Yes, I has a pair o' eyes, and that's just it. If they was a pair o' patent double million magnifyin' microscopes of h'extra power, p'raps I might be able to see up a flight of stairs and through a solid door. But bein' only eyes, you see, my wision's limited!

(*Spectators titter, even the* JUSTICE *smiles.*)

BUZFUZ

(*Trying to conceal his vexation*)

Now, Mr. Weller, I'll ask you a question on another point.

SAM

Relieve yer mind o' whatever's on it. It's all the same to me, as the feller said . . .

(*Catches himself, just as the* JUDGE *starts to reprimand him again.*)

BUZFUZ

(*Sharply*)

Do you remember going up to Mrs. Bardell's house on a subsequent occasion?

SAM

Oh, yes, wery vell.

BUZFUZ

Oh, you *do* remember that, Mr. Weller? I thought we should get at something at last.

SAM

I rayther thought so too, sir.

(*The spectators titter again.*)

BUZFUZ

Well, I suppose you went up to have a little talk about this trial, eh, Mr. Weller?

(*He looks knowingly at the jury.*)

SAM

I went up to pay the rent. But we *did* get a'talkin'.

BUZFUZ

Oh, you did get a-talkin' about the trial. Tell us, Mr. Weller.

SAM

With all the pleasure in life, sir. Arter a few unimportant observations from the two wirtuous females as has been examined here today, the ladies gets into a wery great state o' admiration at the honorable conduct of the legal firm of Dodson and Fogg, and of you in partiklar, Serjeant Buzfuz.

BUZFUZ

(*Pleased*)

Well! They spoke in high praise of the honorable conduct of Messrs. Dodson and Fogg, solicitors of the plaintiff, and of me.

SAM

They did, sir. They said what a wery generous thing it was o' all of you to have taken up this case on spec, and to charge nothin' at all for costs, unless you got 'em out of Mr. Pickwick!

(*The spectators titter again, and* BUZFUZ *looks confused.*)

BUZFUZ

(*To* JUSTICE)

It's perfectly useless, My Lord, attempting to get any evidence through the impenetrable stupidity of this witness. I will not trouble the court by asking him any more questions. Stand down, sir.

SAM

(*Taking up his hat*)

Would any other gentleman like to ask me anythin'?

JUSTICE

Mr. Jerker?

PERKER

No questions, M'lud.

BUZFUZ

(*To* SAM)

You may step down, sir. I shall now call . . .

(SAM *returns to his seat, but, before sitting, waves to someone in the rear.*)

SAM

Greetings, old codger!

BUZFUZ

My Lord, I shall now call my last witness, Mr. Alfred Jingle.

(*There is a great stir at the mention of* JINGLE'S *name—both from* PICKWICK *and some of the spectators.* PICKWICK *springs up to his feet as* JINGLE, *very assured, and peeling off a long and elegant pair of gloves, walks down the aisle.* WARDLE, RACHEL *and the other Pickwickians also rise.*)

PICKWICK

(*To* PERKER)

Jingle! Why is he here?

PERKER

We don't know yet. Very clever, Dodson and Fogg. Particularly Fogg.

USHER

(*Rapping*)

Order! Order!

(*The spectators sit.*)

JINGLE

(*Raising his right hand before the* USHER)

I swear—tell the truth—whole truth—nothing but truth—s'help me God!

(*Kisses the Bible very dramatically and steps into the witness box.*)

PICKWICK

(*Addressing the* JUSTICE)

I object, sir! That person—an impostor, sir!

PERKER

(*Coming over, tugging to pull him back*)

Pickwick, old fellow. Discretion—discretion—strategy.

JUSTICE

(*Rapping his gavel and eyeing* PICKWICK *and* PERKER *severely*)

No further interruption from your client, *please,* Mr. Sherker. (PICKWICK *and* PERKER *return to their seats. The* JUSTICE *turns to* BUZFUZ) Proceed.

BUZFUZ

(*To* JINGLE)

Give the court your name, sir.

JINGLE

Alfred Fitz-Marshall Jingle, Esquire.

JUSTICE

Your occupation, sir?

JINGLE

Many, sir, many.

JUSTICE

Pray, give us *one.*

JINGLE

Of late, sir—a man—of—of *affairs.*

WARDLE

(*From audience*)

Hah! Hah! That's a good one!

(*The* JUSTICE *raises his gavel but does not bring it down.* PICKWICK *sits forward almost bursting with pent-up rage as the scene continues.*)

BUZFUZ

(*To* JINGLE)

You are acquainted with the defendant?

JINGLE

Rather. Know him well. Sporting old boy—heavy drinker—devil with the women.

(PERKER *forcibly holds* PICKWICK *in his chair.*)

BUZFUZ

Ah! A devil with the ladies, you say.

JINGLE

You know—old dog—pretty young girls—at 'em constantly.

(*Turmoil among the spectators.*)

WARDLE

Nonsense!

TUPMAN

Outrageous!

WINKLE

A brazen lie!

SNODGRASS

Shameful!

PICKWICK

(*Springing up, addressing* JUSTICE)

I beg your pardon, sir. But before you give attention to this—this—unreliable p-p-person, I must claim my right to be heard so far as I personally am concerned.

JUSTICE

Hold your tongue, sir!

PICKWICK

(*His voice rising*)

I shall take the liberty of *claiming* my *right* to be . . .

JUSTICE

*(Rapping his gavel)*

Hold your tongue, sir!

*(The other Pickwickians spring up.)*

TUPMAN

Shame! Shame! Give him a hearing!

SNODGRASS

Down with Jingle!

WINKLE

Long live Pickwick! Let him speak! Let him speak!

(PERKER *draws* PICKWICK *back to his seat.*)

JUSTICE

*(Rapping again)*

And I take this occasion to warn the spectators also!

(*Nods to* BUZFUZ.)

BUZFUZ

*(With effort at irony)*

The truth seems to occasion some heat from the defendant's loyal friends. (*Turns back to* JINGLE) And now, sir, could you give us a specific instance of the defendant's licentious nature?

JINGLE

Could give a hundred, sir. Embarrassment of choice. All good.

JUSTICE

Pray give us *one,* sir.

JINGLE

(*Turning to the* JUSTICE *and assuming a sudden diffidence*)

My Lord, I—I'd prefer not. Old gentleman, you see. Matter of taste . . .

JUSTICE

This is a court, sir. We are not concerned with matters of taste.

JINGLE

(*Frowning*)

Loathsome duty—against the grain—but—well, old gentleman offered me ten pounds to hold tongue—refused—question of honor—but . . .

(*Shrugs helplessly.*)

BUZFUZ

Go on, sir.

JINGLE

Defendant here—tried to elope—woman of means—old English stock—fine family—fine girl. Name of Wardle.

(*There is a sudden gasp from* RACHEL.)

WARDLE

Liar! Dog! Slanderer!

(*Rising, waving his stick. The* JUSTICE *pounds for order.*)

JUSTICE

Sit down, sir, or I shall clear the court! (*To* JINGLE) Go on, sir.

PICKWICK

(*Suddenly throwing off* PERKER *and leaping up*)

No! He will *not* go on, sir! This man is an impostor! A blackmailer! A—strolling actor!

JUSTICE

(*Rapping smartly with gavel*)

You are out of order, sir. For the last time, sir—I warn you . . .

PICKWICK

(*Shouting*)

This entire trial is out of order, sir! I say, sir, that of all the disgraceful and rascally proceedings that were ever attempted, this is the most . . .

JUSTICE

(*Rising, shouting*)

Contempt of court, sir. Usher!

PICKWICK

Justice, sir! I demand justice!

PERKER

(*Pleading, tugging at* PICKWICK's *coattails*)

Come, Pickwick—come, I beg you. Sit down.

PICKWICK

(*Jerking away*)

I will not sit down! I'll do nothing, sir! I'll not pay a penny of damages. I'll go to debtors' prison first!

JUSTICE

Indeed you will, sir! Usher, arrest this man!

(*The* USHER *moves toward* PICKWICK. PICKWICK *quickly moves toward* BUZFUZ.)

PICKWICK

(*To* BUZFUZ)

As for you, sir—not one farthing! Not one—farthing—sir! You are all swindlers! Swindlers!

(*By this time the courtroom is in an uproar. The* USHER *is trying to drag off the struggling* PICKWICK. PERKER *is shouting at* BUZFUZ. SAM *is standing on his seat waving his hat and shouting "Hurrah." The* JUSTICE *is beating his gavel.* MRS. BARDELL *and* MRS. CLUPPINS *are shouting at each other.* SNODGRASS, TUPMAN *and* WINKLE *have moved forward and taken up defensive positions near* PICKWICK.)

SNODGRASS

(*Shouting*)

Justice triumphs!

WINKLE

(*Shouting*)

Look before you leap!

TUPMAN

(*Shouting*)

Consider passion!

JUSTICE

(*Pounding frantically with his gavel*)

Usher! Clear the court!

SAM

(*Waving his hat*)

Hurrah!

PICKWICK

(*Shouting above clamor, as the* USHER *drags him away*)

Not one farthing, sir!—not one pound--not one penny!

(*The uproar continues as*

*THE CURTAIN FALLS*

# ACT 2

## SCENE III

*SCENE:* MR. PICKWICK'S *quarters in the Fleet Prison: a small room sparsely furnished with an iron bedstead, chairs, and table. The Pickwickian mottoes—JUSTICE TRIUMPHS, CONSIDER PASSION, LOOK BEFORE YOU LEAP—hang on the wall above the bed.*

*The entrance to the quarters is a barred door, rear. The door is now open, and through it a vista of other prison chambers can be seen in the shadowy distance.*

*AT RISE:* SAM WELLER *is seated on the floor, center, energetically polishing* PICKWICK'S *boots with the aid of muscle and spit.* SAM *appears dejected. At the door, rear, a stout and disreputable* TURNKEY, *with a large ring of keys dangling from his belt and a metal box in one hand, stands sleepily on guard. When the* TURNKEY *has nothing to do—which indeed is most of the time—he jangles his great keys as if to remind all comers that he holds the fate of many men in his hands.*

*No one speaks for several seconds. The* TURNKEY *swings his keys;* SAM *continues his vigorous polishing.*

*After a moment,* MR. TUPMAN, MR. SNODGRASS *and* MR. WINKLE *appear in the doorway. They seem agitated.*

TUPMAN

(*To* TURNKEY)

Your pardon, sir—does a gentleman by the name of Pickwick live . . .

SNODGRASS

Not *live,* Tupman!

TUPMAN

(*Irritably*)

What, then?

SNODGRASS

The man's in *prison,* sir! You should say "held" or "quartered," or . . .

TUPMAN

Quartered, sir! You make it sound as if he'd been *hanged*! Oh, very well—(*He turns again to the* TURNKEY) Is a Mr. Samuel Pickwick quartered . . . (*He breaks off with relief as he catches sight of* PERKER *and* SAM *inside*) Ah, Sam!

(*The three Pickwickians enter quickly;* TUPMAN *carries a bottle under one arm,* WINKLE *a telescope,* SNODGRASS *a sheaf of manuscript.*)

SAM

(*Glumly*)

Velcome to the cage, gentlemen, as the first parrot h'observed on to the second.

TUPMAN

Sam, that keeper fellow—or whoever he is—wouldn't permit us past the front gate until visitors day. Most annoying.

WINKLE

Where *is* the dear man?

SAM

(*Glum, as before*)

Below, sir.

WINKLE

(*Suddenly fearful*)

Be*low?*

TUPMAN

Mercy! Don't tell me . . .

SAM

In the dungeon, sir. A-wisitin' on his feller-debtors and companions in crime.

SNODGRASS

(*Thrilled*)

Dungeon! Companions in crime! A very interesting setting, this.

TUPMAN

Sam, is this where Mr. Pickwick sleeps?

SAM

It 'tis, sir.

WINKLE

Very inadequate, Sam.

TUPMAN

Not at all suitable.

SAM

A wery unsuitable condition, sir.

WINKLE

Sam, when, pray, is Mr. Pickwick returning?

SAM

When the keeper lets him, I suppose.

TUPMAN

Dear me! To think of Mr. Pickwick in a dungeon! How dreadful!

SAM

Just so, sir.

TURNKEY

(*Shaking his tin cup energetically*)

Remember the poor debtors. Remember the poor debtors.

TUPMAN

Bless me! Is that fellow addressing us?

TURNKEY

Sixpence a visitor, if it please ye. Sixpence if it don't.

SNODGRASS

Hadn't we better pay the fellow?

SAM

(*Tossing him a coin*)

There's fer you, old bloater!

(MR. PERKER *enters briskly.*)

PERKER

Good morning, gentlemen, good morning! But what a pity to meet under such conditions.

SNODGRASS

Any progress on the case, Mr. Perker?

PERKER

Great progress, sir.

WINKLE

Oh, very cheering.

TUPMAN

Excellent.

SAM

You means, sir, Mr. Pickwick won't have to cough up the damages?

PERKER

Well—as to that—yes, he probably will, but . . .

SAM

Then whur's the progress?

PERKER

My dear boy, in all legal affairs, when any time passes and matters get no worse, we call that progress. I only hope Mr. Pickwick is prepared to be reasonable. How is his temper today, Sam?

SAM

Wery much like it wuz yesterday and the day before.

PERKER

Ah, good. Now I know what to do. You may depend on me.

(*He goes out.*)

TUPMAN

Poor Pickwick. At least the dear boy's door is unbarred.

WINKLE

Of course, Tupman. Even in prison they recognize a gentleman.

SAM

Bless your h'innocent heart, sir. Only if yer drops yer shillin's regular into the box.

TUPMAN

The box?

SAM

(*Shouting over to the* TURNKEY)

An't thet right, old rumpot?

JINGLE

(*In doorway*)

I say—fellow—turnkey—. Come now—chin up there—problem here—urgent—very. Where's Pickwick?

TUPMAN

Bless me! Mr. Jingle, isn't it?

JINGLE

The same, sir. Though not the same—eh? Never mind—serves me right—bad fate—strange story—downhill—very.

TUPMAN

What are you doing here, sir?

WINKLE

How dare you, sir, present yourself to Mr. Pickwick?

JINGLE

Ah, sir. Hold fire—many changes. Pickwick—Jingle—fellow prisoners—dear friends now—close—very.

SNODGRASS

You are a resident here, sir?

JINGLE

Resident? Ah, charming. Well put. Delicate. Most. Here briefly, sir. Forced stay. Port in storm. Rocky coast. Sit a moment? Don't worry. No bother. Won't talk. Prefer reflection. Some memories good. Forgive appearance. Pawnbroker. Damned rascal. Coat gone. But trousers—good as new, eh?

(*He sits.* PICKWICK, *looking very beamish, enters with* MRS. BARDELL.)

PICKWICK

Ah, most loyal friends. Splendid to see you all.

WINKLE

We've been so concerned about you.

SNODGRASS

To think of you in a dungeon!

PICKWICK

I was only making my morning rounds. I've passed out porridge to all the empty bellies below and continued, at rather close quarters, my studies of human nature. One moment gentlemen, and my full attention is yours. Mr. Turnkey?

TURNKEY

Yes, sir?

PICKWICK

Mrs. Bardell here—Number 21 on the gallery—is in great need of a warming-pan. Will you see that she is supplied?

TURNKEY

One warmin'-pan. Yes, sir.

PICKWICK

Is that all, Mrs. Bardell?

MRS. BARDELL

Everything, sir—and thank 'ee kindly, sir.

TUPMAN

Gracious me! Is Mrs. Bardell also in prison?

SAM

Certainly, sir. Until someone pays the costs of the trial, sir, allays gets paid some way, Dodson and Fogg. Particularly Fogg.

TUPMAN

(*To* PICKWICK)

Am I to believe, sir, that you intend to allow this innocent, if misguided, widow to languish and suffer within these walls just because you refuse to pay?

PICKWICK

Suffer, sir? Did you say suffer?

TUPMAN

I did, sir.

PICKWICK

My dear Tupman, Mrs. Bardell has never been happier. Have you, my dear?

MRS. BARDELL

No, sir.

PICKWICK

Think of it, never before has the good woman had her meals brought in. No cooking or cleaning, no scrubbing, or domestic duties. Her infant son also behind bars—and thereby no longer a source of worry! Where, gentlemen—where in this world could a woman's life be bettered?

SAM

Possibly nowheres, sir—

PICKWICK

Exactly!

SAM

—though there must be some powerful reason for most people preferrin' to remain on the h'exterior!

PICKWICK

But Sam—don't you think we're very comfortable here?

SAM

Um. Wery compact and comfortable—as the father said ven he cut his little boy's head off to cure him o' squintin'.

PICKWICK

(*Ignoring this*)

Here's for your trouble, Mr. Turnkey.

TURNKEY

Bless ye, sir.

(*He goes.*)

PICKWICK

Good day, Mrs. B. Please to look in when the keeper permits.

MRS. BARDELL

Thank 'ee. Thank 'ee, sir.

(*She goes.*)

PICKWICK

Remarkable, isn't it?

TUPMAN

What, dear boy?

PICKWICK

These small privileges. These pleasant quarters. I've observed, with singular astonishment, gentlemen, that money in prison is just what it is on the outside.

SAM

Um. Wery convenient metal, thet—wherever you happens to be. Here, sir.

PICKWICK

What?

SAM

Yer boots.

PICKWICK

Oh. (PICKWICK *comes to* SAM *and allows him to slip on his boots*) Ah, Mr. Jingle! I didn't see you there, sir! I say, where's your coat? (JINGLE *breaks into sobs*) Dear me! What *is* it, sir?

JINGLE

(*Wiping his face elaborately*)

Boyish to cry—can't help it—vest gone—coat gone. Must eat, you know. Awkward—very!

PICKWICK

Well, now, that's easily remedied, sir. (*Pulls out wallet*) Search out the Turnkey and get some new garments at once.

(*Hands* JINGLE *money.*)

JINGLE

(*Pressing his hand*)

Good friend—damned ashamed. Luck to meet you. Otherwise—starve—die—workhouse funeral—drop the curtain! (*He hurries to the door, then turns back*) Reform, sir. Word of honor. Swear it! Bless you. Touched by kindness. Very!

(JINGLE *goes.*)

PICKWICK

'Pon my soul, England is filled with incorrigible characters. Not a bad sort, Jingle—when you come to know him. Shared a chummage ticket with him when I first came here.

TUPMAN

A what, sir?

PICKWICK

A chummage ticket. (*Then pleased by their bewilderment*) Ah, I see you don't know the expression, gentlemen. Prison term. Picked it up in the whistle-shop.

SNODGRASS

The whistle-shop?

PICKWICK

Ah, you don't know *that* one, either! (*He chuckles*) Good. Good.

TUPMAN

Oh, come, Pickwick, you don't deceive us. We know how wretched you are, sir.

PICKWICK

You do, sir?

SNODGRASS

But how excessively we admire your bold and courageous stand.

(PICKWICK *regards* SNODGRASS *with irony.*)

WINKLE

We have recorded it all, sir!

TUPMAN

Every line!

SNODGRASS

And syllable!

PICKWICK

Well! And—does it make good reading?

SNODGRASS

It is history, sir!

WINKLE

Stone tablets could not say more, sir.

PICKWICK

I am gratified, gentlemen. Deeply gratified.

(*Again he looks grave and thoughtful.*)

TUPMAN

And now, sir, I hope this bottle of cordial . . .

(*Hands his gift over.*)

PICKWICK

How thoughtful, my dear Tupman.

WINKLE

And possibly your telescope . . .

PICKWICK

Ah, yes. Very useful, Winkle. Very.

SNODGRASS

And possibly this poem, sir—a succinct quatrain of my own which I have taken the liberty of dedicating to you . . .

PICKWICK

I am honored, dear Snodgrass.

SNODGRASS

It is quite simply rendered.

PICKWICK

Indeed, I would not have expected it to be otherwise.

SNODGRASS

Shall I read the title?

PICKWICK

Pray do.

SNODGRASS

It is called—"Ode to a Noble Friend in Some Distress, Languishing Betimes in the Fleet Prison by Reason of Certain Unforeseen Misadventures and Fateful Happenings Occurring In and Around the Towns of Stroud, Rochester, Brompton, Chatham—*and* London."

(*An awesome pause.*)

PICKWICK

(*Finally*)

Snodgrass, dear fellow—what can I say? Your inspired title makes me look forward to reading the quatrain itself!

SAM

(*Suddenly, from doorway*)

Whoops! They're a-comin', sir! Whoops!

(*He starts at once in a great flurry to straighten his jacket, his hair, etc.*)

PICKWICK

Good heavens, Sam! Are you having a seizure, my boy?

SAM

No! Yes! *Possibly,* sir!

*(Then, unaccountably,* SAM *suddenly becomes calm, sits, and appears totally unconcerned. They all stare at him. A moment later,* MARY *appears in the doorway.)*

MARY

Good day, gentlemen.

PICKWICK

Bless my soul, Mary! What brings you here, my dear?

SAM

*(Very off-hand)*

Yes, vot a surprise. Yer comin' to see me.

MARY

To see *you,* Mister Weller? Do tell. My business is with Mr. Pickwick. (*To* PICKWICK) Beggin' yer pardon, sir—my mistress is outside.

PICKWICK

*(Flustered, pleased)*

Miss Wardle here? How kind! How excessively kind! Pray—pray show her in, my dear!

MARY

Yes, sir. (*Then coyly to* SAM) Good day, Mister Weller.

*(She slips out quickly.)*

SAM

*(Calling after her)*

Whoa there! Stop the coach! Hold! (*Then agitated, to* PICKWICK) Sir, seein' as how yer h'occupied, could I—a . . .

PICKWICK

Certainly, Sam.

SAM

Thank 'ee, sir! (*He rushes for the door where he turns back quickly*) Yer nightcap, sir!

PICKWICK

What about it?

SAM

Wery becomin', sir—but it's still on yer head!

PICKWICK

Bless me! So it is! (*He jerks off the nightcap.* SAM *hurries out*) Gentlemen, will you forgive me if—if—Miss Wardle and I . . .

(*The three Pickwickians exchange a glance of distress.*)

TUPMAN

(*Crossing to the wall*)

Pickwick, your life is your own, sir, but *this* time, pray . . . (*He points to the sign*) LOOK BEFORE YOU LEAP!

WINKLE

(*Crossing to the wall*)

*And* . . . (*He points to the sign*) CONSIDER PASSION! Pickwick married is a Pickwick lost.

SNODGRASS

(*Holding up an admonishing finger*)

Remember—the Club!

(MISS WARDLE *enters.*)

MISS WARDLE

(*Advancing with outstretched hand*)

Oh, sir, my warmest, most heartfelt sympathies to you in this hour of need!

PICKWICK

(*Touched*)

Dear Miss Wardle!

SNODGRASS

(*Bowing gravely and brushing past* RACHEL)

Miss Wardle . . .

(SNODGRASS *goes out.*)

WINKLE

(*Bowing*)

Miss Wardle—

(WINKLE *goes out.*)

TUPMAN

(*Bowing*)

Miss Wardle—(TUPMAN *goes to the door, pauses*) We shall be outside, Pickwick, if you need our *help!*

(TUPMAN *goes out. A pause.* RACHEL WARDLE *regards the room.*)

RACHEL

Bars! Bars! Oh, sir, I do trust your impetuous and gallant spirit has not been broken by incarceration!

PICKWICK

Not a whit, ma'am.

RACHEL

Your innocence, sir, is now understood by *every* Wardle!

PICKWICK

Your understanding is most touching.

(*He takes her hand.*)

RACHEL

(*Drawing away quickly*)

Oh, sir, pray do not be ardent again!

PICKWICK

(*Startled*)

Why not, dear girl? My admiration for you . . .

RACHEL

Oh, sir, you bring me shrewdly to the subject of my visit! (*She averts her eyes*) I cannot deceive you, sir—our mutual interest exists no longer.

PICKWICK

Indeed?

RACHEL

Science, sir—science has lost its hold on me!

PICKWICK

(*Shocked*)

No!

RACHEL

Yes, Mr. Pickwick! I freely admit it!

PICKWICK

But Miss Wardle—your—moths . . .

RACHEL

Abandoned, sir! Every moth—*gone*!

PICKWICK

Ma'am, you amaze me! *If* there was *anything* that set you apart, if there was *anything* . . .

RACHEL

Mr. Pickwick, I beg you, allow me to speak further!

PICKWICK

Speak, ma'am, speak. There must be more to say!

RACHEL

(*Turning away*)

There is! Oh, how can I convey my true feelings! Mr. Pickwick, my very heart has flown!

PICKWICK

Dear me! To what? To whom?

RACHEL

To a person, sir—with a soul!

PICKWICK

Indeed! I should like to see such a person.

RACHEL

You *shall,* sir! He begged to accompany me. He is here. (RACHEL *steps to the door and calls*) Come, dear guide and counselor—enter!

(*After a moment* MR. STIGGINS, *aided by the* TURNKEY, *enters uncertainly.*)

PICKWICK

(*Stunned*)

Mr. Stiggins! Bless me!

MR. STIGGINS

(*Rolling his eyes heavenward*)

Sts—sts—sts—this wicked world! Oh, sir, the accursed cruelty of your inhuman persecutors!

(*He covers a hiccough.*)

How terrible! These cold prison walls.

(*He sees the bottle and his eye brightens.*)

Ahh! How necessary!

(*He swoops up the bottle and heads for the door.*)

Come, dear lady. Must extend our blessings without delay to the keeper of these wounded souls.

(*He goes out.* PICKWICK, *bewildered, stares after him.*)

RACHEL

Farewell, Mr. Pickwick. I know my news has been the rudest shock to you. But Time, Time, sir, will assuage the pain and scars. Be brave, sir.

PICKWICK

I shall make every effort, ma'am.

(MISS WARDLE *leaves.* PICKWICK *is alone for a moment. The three Pickwickians look through the door cautiously and then enter with* SAM.)

SAM

Vell, so vot happened sir?

TUPMAN

Yes, Pickwick, what?

PICKWICK

Gentlemen, Miss Wardle is lost to me forever. She has found another interest more congenial to her spirit.

(*The Pickwickians all look pleased.*)

SNODGRASS

Sir, I congratulate you! You have considered passion . . .

WINKLE

And emerged victorious!

TUPMAN

No doubt, sir, you exerted the greatest will to resist Miss Wardle's . . .

SNODGRASS

Unquestionable charms!

WINKLE

Gentlemen, let us once more surround our leader's name with a rich halo . . .

(*At this moment* MR. PERKER *rushes in.*)

PERKER

(*Very excited*)

Mr. Pickwick! Mr. Pickwick! Mr. Buzfuz is coming through the prison yard. He wishes to see you.

TUPMAN

Buzfuz himself!

SNODGRASS

Splendid!

WINKLE

How hopeful!

PERKER

Well, sir, what do you say?

PICKWICK

(*Thoughtfully*)

Mr. Perker, I should welcome the chance to see Mr. Buzfuz again.

PERKER

Excellent! I'll fetch him at once. At once! (*He hurries to the cell doorway and calls*) Mr. Buzfuz—Mr. Buzfuz! Mr. Pickwick is—a—ready—to . . .

(BUZFUZ *enters.*)

BUZFUZ

Ah, Mr. Pickwick. I trust you are well, sir? (*A pause*) I don't think you are looking quite as stout as when I had the pleasure of seeing you last.

PICKWICK

You think not, sir?

BUZFUZ

No, not nearly as stout.

PERKER

(*Quickly*)

Mr. Buzfuz, I think you'll find my client very agreeably disposed to—er . . .

BUZFUZ

(*To* PICKWICK)

Gratified that you've chosen to be sensible, Mr. Pickwick. Very awkward and expensive, these legal matters. Eh, gentlemen?

(*He acknowledges the presence of the other Pickwickians.*)

TUPMAN

(*Coldly*)

Very.

BUZFUZ

(*Drawing out some papers*)

Now, sir—everything has been prepared. Just sign these papers, pay your damages, and you'll be free to return to society like a responsible fellow.

PICKWICK

(*Bristling*)

Responsible fellow, am I, sir?

BUZFUZ

I believe you are, sir—at heart!

PICKWICK

(*His voice rising*)

And *you,* sir—what are *you* at heart, sir? . . . I'll tell you, sir—you are a mean, rascally, villainous, heartless robber, sir!

BUZFUZ

*(Startled by this unexpected onslaught)*

Sir!

PERKER

*(To* BUZFUZ, *with forced gaiety)*

He! He! He! You see? That's all there is to it, sir! You're a heartless robber, Mr. Buzfuz. He! He! He! Come long with me now and . . .

(PERKER, *aided by* SAM *and* MARY, *nudges the angry* BUZFUZ *toward the door.)*

BUZFUZ

*(Protesting, turning back)*

You must pay the costs, sir! *(To* PERKER) The costs! Do you hear?

PICKWICK

*(Raging, following after him)*

Pay the costs, sir! Pay for your swindling, lying, deceitful, avaricious jiggery-pokery! You're a robber, sir, and a villain—and a mean, rascally fellow, sir. Get out—before I lose my temper!

(SAM *and* PERKER *have* BUZFUZ *off by now.* PICKWICK *hurries to the door, shouting after him)*

Robber, sir! *Robber! Robber! (He turns back to his friends, shaking with anger. Suddenly his usual benign expression returns)* Honest indignation, gentlemen. Nothing more. But I do feel a great deal better for having expressed myself!

*(A pause)*

Gentlemen, you *do* think, don't you, that Mr. Buzfuz got my point?

SNODGRASS

I'm inclined to believe he did, sir.

WINKLE

Of course you realize, sir, this means you will remain in prison indefinitely.

PICKWICK

(*His eyes lighting up*)

Do you really think so?

TUPMAN

I do, sir!

(*At this moment,* SAM, *very disheveled, enters with* MARY, *who follows him brushing his clothes.* SAM *carries a sheaf of papers in his hand.* MARY *gazes at him proudly.*)

SAM

Wery extraordinary thing, sir!

PICKWICK

Dear me, Sam! Did you meet with an accident?

SAM

In a manner o' speakin', yessir! (*He hands the papers to* PICKWICK) Here, sir. Mr. Buzfuz wants to return these 'ere signed papers,

(PICKWICK *and the others stare*)

drop the costs of the trial, free Missus Bardell, and h'arrange everything most agreeable. Wery extraordinary thing!

(*He dusts his clothes again.*)

WINKLE

But—that's very puzzling, Sam. A few moments ago . . .

SAM

Wery puzzlin', sir.

PICKWICK

(*Suddenly, severely*)

Sam, did you have a hand in this sudden settlement?

SAM

Vell, sir, to be honest—for a brief space I had *both* hands in it!

PICKWICK

(*Shocked*)

Sam! You struck Mr. Buzfuz!

SAM

Oh, no, sir—I oney had my arm greatly h'extended as the gentleman rapidly approached me! . . .

(PICKWICK *eyes him severely.*)

TUPMAN

And the papers, Sam?

SAM

Well, sir, thet's the h'ingenious part of it, sir! Let's just say—between us all everythin' wuz wrote out proper.

MARY

Mister Weller wuz wonderful, sir!

SAM

(*Pleased*)

Comin' from you, my dear, the compliment is hereby h'accepted—and you gets yer receipt fer it stamped and delivered herewith!

(*He kisses her promptly.*)

PICKWICK

(*Staring*)

Bless me! (*When the embrace continues,* PICKWICK *crosses and taps* SAM *on the arm*) Sam! (SAM *ignores him and* PICKWICK *pulls his sleeve*) Sam!

SAM

(*Finally breaking away*)

You wuz speakin' guv'nor?

PICKWICK

My boy, I am sorry to interrupt your—your activities, but I must know exactly what your deplorable methods with Mr. Buzfuz accomplished?

TUPMAN

Accomplished! Pickwick, don't you understand, you're free!

PICKWICK

I am?

SAM

Yessir. You're out o' the cage right now!

PICKWICK

(*After a pause*)

Well, gentlemen, I suppose I should be very happy, but, I can't say I haven't enjoyed it here. These experiences have added immeasurably to my knowledge and understanding.

WINKLE

How gratifying it is, Pickwick, to see once again that justice triumphs!

SNODGRASS

Indeed, yes. Another trial and another victory!

(MRS. BARDELL *hurries in*)

MRS. BARDELL

Oh, sir—Mr. Perker jest told me the news, so will you be comin' home fer supper?

MR. PICKWICK

Supper? Why not? All of us.

MRS. BARDELL

I'll have everything ready fer you, sirs. Would ye be likin' anythin' special fer supper, sir?

MR. PICKWICK

No, just the usual, Mrs. Bardell. Chops and toma—

(*He breaks off abruptly, then looks hard at her*)

Better make it kidney pie!

(*He heads for the door quickly.*)

*THE CURTAIN FALLS*